BACK TO BASICS

How to Help Congregations Get Back to God's Priorities

J.J. TURNER, PH.D.

Published by
Solutions 2.0. Inc.
McDonough, GA 30252

12 REASONS FOR GOING BACK TO BASICS

(Identify your agreement or disagreement by checking **Yes or No**)

1. The Christian's walk and the church's mission both started with the basics, basics we need to return to from time to time. [ ] Yes [ ] No
2. Returning to basics remind us and reaffirm our original commitment to Christ and the mission of the church. [ ] Yes [ ] No
3. Going back to basics strengthens the foundation. [ ] Yes [ ] No
4. You can't stay on the mission given by God if you don't know the basics, which we need to return to from time to time. [ ] Yes [ ] No
5. Going back to basics reminds us of why we are doing what we are doing today. [ ] Yes [ ] No
6. Going back to basics reminds us of how blessed we are today to be building on such a powerful heritage. [ ] Yes [ ] No
7. The basics must not be forgotten, neglected, or thought of as antiques; we must continue to build on them every day. [ ] Yes [ ] No
8. Going back to basics will help us adjust or change where we have strayed. [ ] Yes [ ] No
9. Satan wants us to forget the place and power of the basics which we have, and are, building on today. [ ] Yes [ ] No
10. A congregation which is not building on the basics given by God is not pleasing to God. [ ] Yes [ ] No
11. Back to basics strengthen our core values. [ ] Yes [ ] No
12. Every member must be educated and re-educated in the basics upon which the mission of the church resides. [ ] Yes [ ] No

WHEN WAS THE LAST TIME YOU STUDIED THE BASICS?

"Will You not REVIVE us again, that your people may rejoice in You? Show us mercy, LORD, and grant us your salvation"

(Psalm 85:6, 7).

CONTENT

PREFACE

Welcome to the exciting, refreshing, and faith-building series of lessons on basic biblical truths and doctrine related specifically to the basic and core mission of the church and the **E's,** (memory tools), which support the mission.

No! This is not another study of "mission work" as we usually think about it. It's not a study on the selection, supporting, and sending of a man and his family to the mission field beyond our borders whom we call "our missionaries."   There is nothing wrong with this; in fact, we need more and more missionaries. The world population is growing while our "sending population" is declining. We must pray for *"The Lord of the harvest to send forth workers."*

I venture to say you could never guess how much interest there is in creating or crafting a church mission statement. Today I typed in "Mission Statement" in Google search and 945,000,000 results popped up. Obviously, there is more than a casual interest in this subject; there is mega interest.

A Wikipedia article on this subject gives an extensive definition of what constitutes a Mission Statement: *"A mission statement typically is a short statement of why an organization exists, what its overall goal is, identifying the goal of its operations; what kind of product or service it provides, its primary customers or market, and its geographical region of operation"* (Wikipedia. Org/wiki/missionstatement).

In this study the overall mission of the church is identified as *glorifying God and Christ in the church (Ephesians 3:21);* and the **E's** as extensions of ways we glorify God in the local church.

This study in new, practical, enlightening, biblical, and much needed by every congregation as well as every member. It will help clarify any possible misunderstandings, which there are many, related to the mission of the church. It is obvious we cannot pursue the church's mission in its fullness if we don't know what it is.

The overriding objective of this study is to present a challenge to balance the factors involved in fulfilling the amazing and biblical mission of the Lord's church, which we are all privileged and blessed to participate in. It advocates "doing the word", not just knowing it.

If these basics aren't in place it will be difficult, if not impossible, to move on to studying and applying the truths about worship, leadership, stewardship, and other basics essential to a healthy church. We'll be addressing "first things first"—CORE basics.

There is a *"For Thought and Discussion"* section after each lesson designed to contribute to the study and application of the lesson. Every member of the church needs a copy of this book to read and study as well as an opportunity to study it in a group. Teens need it too. It would also be a great study for those who are preparing themselves to become Christians. It is essential to "counting the cost" so there will be no surprises later (Cf. Matthew 16:24).

[This study has 3 major parts related to "Back to Basics"]

Introduction

"DRIFTING ALONG WITH THE TUMBLING TUMBLEWEED"

When I was a boy one of my favorite songs was, Drifting Along With The Tumbling Tumble Weed, sung by the *Sons of the Pioneer,* and featured in numerous cowboy movies. This historical memory popped into my awareness as I was thinking about how to introduce this material.

My question was, "How did the church, at least many congregations, become so far removed from the basics given by God?" Among my choices, and the word chosen was DRIFT. Starting back with the thirty-plus churches mentioned in the New Testament, none of which exists today; not even the historical Jerusalem church. They didn't one day get up and affirm, "Starting today we are going to do our own thing; it doesn't matter what God says." It happened over time.

I believe the biblical evidence, as well as historical evidence, supports it happened over a period of time involving drifting, which may have started gradually and then gained momentum. Congregations at that time in history didn't flip a switch and become 100% removed from the basics established by the Lord. It occurred by drifting along with the tumbling tumbleweed. Inch by inch.

The evidence and consequences of drifting are not limited to the Lord's church. It is seen in the culture of our society. It seems to be a tendency of human nature. In his book *titled, Slouching Toward Gomorrah,* Robert H. Bork wrote:

"With each new evidence of deterioration, we lament for a moment, and then become accustomed to it…. So unrelenting is the assault on our sensibilities that many of us grow numb, finding resignation to be rational, adaptive response to an environment that is increasingly polluted and apparently beyond control….As behavior worsens, the community adjusts its standards to that conduct once thought reprehensible but is no longer deemed so." (p.2, 1996, New York, N.Y. HarperCollins).

BIBLICAL EXAMPLES OF CHURCHES DRIFTING

A clear Bible model of a congregation drifting away from the basics established by God is the church of the *"foolish Galatians"*. It is believed that Paul established several congregations during his first preaching journey (A.D. 45-48) in the region of Galatia in Central Asia Minor (Read Acts 13 & 14).

A few years later (about A.D. 57) Paul writes the church in Galatia and documents his concerns: *"I am astonished that you are so QUICKLY DISERTING the One who called you by the Grace of Christ and are turning to a different gospel" (Galatians 1:6)…. "You foolish Galatians! Who has bewitched you?" (3:1-3).*

When the subject of drifting churches and departing from the faith, the 7 Churches of Asia come to mind; especially the five that were in trouble with the Head of the church—Christ Himself. Remember the church in Ephesus? Paul wrote an epistle to them in which he encouraged them to grow and keep the unity of the Spirit (Cf. chapter 4). Later, Christ, the head and Savior of the church made this diagnosis of the church's spiritual condition: *"You have LEFT your first love"* (Revelation 2:4).

It is also obvious that the epistle to the Hebrews also identifies issues which were failures, signs of drifting, and the need for renewal. The church had been in existence for a number of years and had been strong (10:32; 13:7; 2:3), but now, *"In fact, though by this time you ought to be teachers, you need someone to teach you the elementary truths of God's word all over again"* (Hebrews 5:12). Back in 2:1, they had been warned, *"We must pay more careful attention, therefore, to what we have HEARD, so that we do not DRIFT away"* (NIV).

The Greek word translated DRIFT is <u>pararrein.</u> It has several meanings in classical Greek: *"To flow beside, to glide aside from, to fall off, decline and to make a forfeit of faith; something that is slipping away."* Picture the docking of a boat and then because it is not properly secured, watched, or attention given to the wind and rising tide it drifts from the dock. The church, as well as each member, must be properly CONNECTED to Christ by the basic mooring lines of truth, etc.

Think and meditate on this truth. The churches we read about in the New Testament, taught and led by the Apostles over the period covered in the book Acts, drifted away so completely they ceased to exist. Then as we march through history from the 2nd –Century to today in the 21s-Century we have an ever-growing record-book filled with the stories of how congregations DRIFTED away from Christ and the Gospel. This happened because moorings to the basics taught and commanded by God's word were neglected, changed, and abandoned.

Since the Bible documents the drift and departures of churches and Christians from the basics in the 1st-Century, we should not be surprised to see it happening today. The drifting of a church from the basics is gradual and moves in cycles. Departure from core (original) beliefs, practices (in worship), and reduction and neglect of the mission doesn't happen overnight or from an edict quickly rendered in a business meeting.

Think about this portion of Scripture and what it has to contribute to our subject of drifting from the basics. **Judges 2:7-11:**

*"So the people served the Lord all the days of Joshua, and all the days of the elders who outlived Joshua, who had seen all the great works of the Lord which he had done for Israel. Now Joshua the son of Nun, the servant of the Lord, died when he was one hundred and ten years old. And they buried him within the border in his inheritance at Timnath Heres, in the mountains of Ephraim, on the north side of Mount Gaash. When all that generation had been gathered to their fathers, another generation arose from them **who did not know the Lord nor the work which He had done for Israel.** Then the children of Israel did evil in the sight of the Lord, and served Baal."*

As noted in the First-Century Churches the drift starts by the attitude, beliefs, and actions of the first members, and as we see in the case of Israel it may start when the next generation is in charge and departs from the basics. Remember this history is written and preserved from our knowledge and learning (Cf. Romans 15:4).

[Remember the **E's** are memory tools for association and keys for learning the lessons]

FOR THOUGHT AND DISCUSSION

1. Share some of your observations relative to how you've seen congregations drift from the basics? Why did they?

2. Read Revelation 2:1-7. Why do you suppose the church had *"left its first love"*? What was the basic age of the church?

3. Read Hebrews 2:1-4; from what were those Christians drifting?

4. Discuss why Paul referred to the Galatians as "foolish"?

5. In your opinion what are some of the easier things for a church to drift from? Why?

6. What additional observations do you have?

7. How will you intentionally apply this lesson to your life and ministry?

Part 1

BASICS ABOUT THE CHURCH

Lesson 1

FIRST THINGS FIRST

Years ago I would frequently see benches at bus stops with this sign painted on the backrest: "Attend the Church of Your Choice." That sign, even though biblically it was contrary to Scripture, was preferred to signs about alcohol, tobacco, and certain R-rated movies. That sign was a typical representation back then, as well as now, of the concept and lack of knowledge most people, and yes some even in the church, have relative to the identity and mission of the church.

After I got out of the Navy I got a job as a machinist in a factory. About the only thing I knew about the business of the factory was how to spell the word and locate its address. But through a patient owner and education by a gracious foreman, I learned the basics of the company and was able to advance quicker than was normally expected from a new worker. Knowing and building on the basics made the difference.

My point is that you can't effectively and efficiently accomplish the mission of the church if you don't know, understand, and apply the basics which are foundational to the success of God's eternal plan for the church (Cf. Ephesians 1:3-7). Our study is about back to basics. Okay, where do we start?

We start with the first thing being FIRST. This first thing is the English word CHURCH. It may, or may not, surprise some that the word church is misunderstood and used in various ways, not only by outsiders but by Christians too.

The most obvious misunderstanding is that the "church is a building"; second, the church is a specific place where God resides and you have to go there to worship Him; and third, the church is a social group that is negative and against "having fun and enjoying the pleasures earned in life." Even some of Webster's definitions don't harmonize with what the Bible says, it relies on "popular use."

LET THE BIBLE SPEAK ABOUT CHURCH

In order to properly, biblically, and actively understand the mission of the church, we must have a biblical awareness and understanding of the nature of the church as given by God in Scripture. What follows is a brief overview of what Jesus said about His church:

And understanding begins with Jesus' promise in Matthew 16:

When Jesus came into regions of Caesarea Philippi, He asked His disciples, saying, 'Who do men say that I am?' So they said, 'Some say John the Baptist, some Elijah, and others Jeremiah or one of the prophets.' He said unto them, 'But who do you say that I am?' Simon Peter answered and said, 'You are the Christ, the Son of the living God.' Jesus answered and said unto him, 'Blessed are you, Simon Bar-Jonah, for flesh and blood has not revealed this unto you, but My Father who is in heaven. And I say to you that you are Peter, and on this ROCK I will BUILD MY CHURCH, and the gates of Hades shall not prevail against it. And I will give you the keys to the kingdom of heaven, and whatever you bind on earth will be bound in heaven, and whatever you loose on earth will be loosed in heaven.' Then He commanded His disciples that they should tell no one that He was Jesus the Christ" (Matthew 16:13-20).

A CLOSER LOOK AT JESUS' PROMISE

It is beyond the scope of this study to do a full in-depth exegesis of Jesus' promise to build His church. Here is a quick outline of His promise:

1. The promise to BUILD centers in His divinity, ability, integrity and mission given to Him by his Father. It was very personal, *"I will build'*; **not men, companies, councils, governments, etc.**

2. **"MY CHURCH"** refers to possession and ownership; no one or group would be given the task of building His church.

3. The keyword is **CHURCH.** It is unfortunate and unbiblical that men have applied the word to a physical structure (building). The Greek word used by Jesus is *ekklesia*, which was understood to refer to a *"calling out for a purpose; to gather or assemble for a specific cause or reason.* According to Scripture, we have been *called by the Gospel (2 Thessalonians 2:14).* We have been called out of the world which involves us coming together from time to time in an assembly (Hebrews 10:24, 25). The *EKKLESIA* refers to PEOPLE, not a physical place.

4. Another keyword is **ROCK**; it is the Greek word *petra* which refers to a large rock formation, to bedrock in contrast to a pebble which is the rock Peter was referred to by Jesus. The Jews were familiar with ROCK in reference to God—He was the Rock In his letter to the Corinthians, Paul affirmed that Jesus was the

ROCK that followed Israel in the wilderness: *"[A]nd all drank the same spiritual drink. For they drank the spiritual Rock that followed them, and that ROCK WAS CHRIST"* (1 Corinthians 10:4). The Psalmist wrote, *"I will love You, O Lord, my strength. The Lord is my ROCK and my fortress and my deliverer; My God, my strength, in whom I will trust"* (Psalm 18:1, 2). David acknowledged that God was the Rock: *"The Lord is my ROCK and my fortress and my deliverer; the God of my strength, in whom I will trust"* (2 Samuel 22:2, 3). Jesus' church is built on the foundation of Him being God (Cf. 1 Corinthians 3:9-17).

5. Jesus promised that the **gates of Hades** would not stop or prevent Him from calling out people to follow Him. Jesus was referring to the fact that His death and burial would not prevent or stop Him from calling out a people through the Gospel (Read Acts 2:24; 1 Peter 3:18; Romans 1:14-16).

6. Jesus promised *"The **keys to the kingdom of heaven"*** would be given, which meant authority to preach the "reign and rule of God" with a promised destination of heaven to the obedient. Peter was chosen to preach—issue the Gospel call—the first Gospel sermon after Jesus ascension to heaven. The call (ekklesia) resulted in 3000 people being **called out** by the Gospel (Acts 2).

A biblical understanding of the nature of the church (*ekklesia*) is absolutely essential to carrying out the mission of the church. How is

It or would it be possible to fulfill the "Great Commission" given to the church if we don't know the true nature and identify of the called out people of God? This should be an incentive to spend some quality time studying what the Bible has revealed about the *ekklesia (church).*

FOR THOUGHT AND DISCUSSION

1. Why do some people, maybe even most, think of the church as a building or physical location?

2. How much study have you given to the Greek word *ekklesia*?

3. Do you know why King James insisted that "church" be the translation of *ekklesia and* not translated "assembled, assembly, or the gathered"?

4. Why is it essential that we have a biblical understanding of the church in order to carry out the mission assigned by Christ?

5. Why must **back to basics** include the study of the church?

6. Why does the Catholic Church claim Peter was the first Pope?

7. What question or observation do you have?

8. How will you intentionally apply this lesson to your life and ministry?

Lesson 2

UNDERSTANDING CHURCH AS A COMMUNITY

It is not enough to understand basically that the church in the First Century was a group of *"called out"* people; called out for a purpose. In order to participate and fulfill the mission of the church, we must have an understanding of what was the reality and purpose of the *"assembled or gathered people."* Why were they "called out"?

Here's the bottom line for this study. The **ekklesia** was the word used by the Holy Spirit in the First Century to identify sinners who were called by the Gospel to form a new community of people. They were called out of darkness into light; they were moved from having no hope to having eternal hope; they were moved from no identity to a new identity; from being without family to be adopted into the family of God. All of these blessings and more were possible only in the called-out community which we call "church" today.

The idea for a new community wasn't an afterthought, as some advocate today who believe Jesus failed to accomplish His mission of setting up a physical kingdom. The prophets of Israel predicted that God would call out a new community in the latter days, and the calling would be accomplished by His Son and his followers—the church.

Here are some of those prophecies:

1. Isaiah prophesied of the coming of a future community which would have as a goal the inclusion of all people: *"Now it shall come to pass in the latter days that the mountain of the Lord's house shall be established on the top of the mountains, and shall be exalted about the hills, and ALL NATIONS shall flow unto it"* (Isaiah 2:2).

2. Isaiah also predicted that the future community would be composed of people who invited others to join them: *"Many people shall come and say, 'Come, and let us go up to the mountain of the Lord, to the house of the God of Jacob...'"* (Isaiah 2:3).

3. The prophecy also contained the promise of the future community would be characterized by teaching: *"He will teach us His ways, and we shall walk in His Paths. For out of Zion shall go forth the law, and the word of the Lord from Jerusalem"* (Isaiah 2:3).

Jesus promised that the ekklesia (new community) would have residents from all over the earth: *"They will come from the EAST and WEST, from the NORTH and SOUTH, and sit down in the kingdom of God. And indeed there are last who will be first, and there are first who will be last"* (Luke 13:29, 30).

Jesus announced that He had sheep which were not of the "fold of Israel": *"And other sheep I have which ARE NOT of this fold; them also I MUST BRING, and they will hear My voice, and there will be ONE flock*

One Shepherd" (John 10:16). John announced that Jesus *"was the Lamb of God who would take away the sins of the WORLD" (John 1:29).*

Jesus tasted of death for EVERYBODY: *"But we see Jesus, who was made a little lower than the angels, for the suffering of death crowned with glory and honor, that He, by the grace of God, might taste of DEATH for EVERYONE" (Hebrews 2:9).*

In a parable stressing the global invitation to all men to come to the master's banquet, Jesus said, *"Then the master said to the servant, 'Go out into the highways and hedges, and COMPEL them to come it, that my HOUSE may be filled" (Luke 14:23; Cf. 1 Timothy 3:15,*the church is referred to as a house).

The apostle Paul, in harmony with Hosea's prophecy, said the Gentiles were "grafted into the body of Christ" and became one with the Jews who were in Christ—both formed ONE COMMUNITY (Read Romans chapter 11; and book of Hosea).

To churches suffering persecution the apostle John was given this message relative to the identity of members: *"After these things I looked, and behold, a great multitude, which no one could number, of ALL NATIONS, TRIBES, and PEOPLES. TONGUES, standing before the throne and before the Lamb, clothed with white robes, with palm branches in their hands" (Revelation 7:9)*

The new community would be identified by LOVE. First love for God, others, and self (Mark 12:28-34). Like now, back then it was a "dog eat dog" world. This is why it would be an amazing and undeniable sign when Jesus' community was recognized and known for their *"love for one another" (John 13:34, 35).* Why they were even to *"love their enemies" (Matthew 5:43-48).* In 1st Corinthians 13, Paul outlined a set of attitudes and behaviors which would be demonstrated by love; which was the solution to all their problems. Among all virtues love was the GREATEST (1 Corinthians 13: 11-13).

The called-out community would be under constant scrutiny by outsiders. Therefore, they must, as "resident aliens" conduct themselves properly. Peter wrote: *"But let none of you suffer as a murderer, a thief, an evildoer, or as a busy body in other people's matters. Yet if anyone suffers as a Christian, let him not be ashamed, but let him glorify God in this matter" (1 Peter 4:15, 16).*

The called-out community in the 1st Century had a clear and specific identity. It was not (1) a building, (2) name on a building, (3) location, (4) financial standing, (5) popular preacher, (6) elaborate programs, or (7) involvement in political affairs. Christians in the 1st Century were identified by their LOVE AND CARE FOR EACH OTHER, as well as their benevolence toward outsiders (C. James 1:27; Galatians 6:10; Acts 6).

To the hurting, downtrodden, confused, and lonely; Jesus gave them a gracious invitation: *"Come to Me, ALL YOU who labor and are heavy laden, and I WILL give you rest"* (Matthew 11:28). He promised heaven to those troubled in the heart (John 14:1-4). Who wouldn't want to accept such gracious promises?

The called-out community didn't shun, avoid, or think anyone was too bad for membership in the body of Christ. "Only Sinners were eligible for membership." Jesus said, *"I came not to call the righteous to repentance but sinners."* In reminding the Corinthians of the gift of eternal life and salvation, Paul wrote: *"Do you not know that the unrighteous will not inherit the kingdom of God? Do not be deceived. Neither fornicators, nor idolaters, nor adulterers, nor homosexuals, nor sodomites, nor thieves, nor covetous, nor drunkards, nor revilers, nor extortioners will inherit the kingdom of God. And SUCH WERE SOME OF YOU.* **BUT** *you were WASHED, but you were JUSTIFIED in the name of the Lord Jesus and by the SPIRIT OF GOD"* (1 Corinthians 6:9, 10).

The world of the First Century, just like the world of today, was presenting an ever luring power to pursue a place of acceptance. Today the allure of capitalism, consumerism, elitism, and success at any cost are unquestionable "virtues" desired by both the lost and saved, those in and out of the church. Everybody wants the tree of knowledge.

Based on the previous Scriptures we have noticed; some of God's objectives (goals) for His *ekklesia (called out community)* are as follows:

1. God's objective is for the cultural difference to contribute to the "unity of the Spirit and the bond of peace"; not segregation or isolation (Cf. Ephesians 4:1-10).
2. God's objective is not for socioeconomics to make a difference in a member's acceptance or recognition in the body of Christ.

Paul said the stewardship of giving is based not on an amount but on the status of the heart: *"For if there is FIRST a willing mind, it is acceptable according to what one has, and not according to what he does not have" (2 Corinthians 8:12).*

3. We have noticed that geographical differences and ethnic backgrounds do not constitute a privileged status in the body of Christ. Read 1 Corinthians 12:12-31. Relational preferences must not foster "clicks" and isolation into small groups within small groups—"Me and my four and no more" is not acceptable.

4. Striving, arguing, and division over theological questions, especially those which aren't clear and are based only on traditions, must be avoided. Paul warned Timothy about such traps: *"As I urged you when I went into Macedonia—remain in Ephesus that you may charge some that teach no other doctrine, nor give heed to fables and endless genealogies, which cause dispute rather than godly edification which is in faith" (1 Timothy 1:3, 4).*

5. The mission of the church is not to set up tribunals that have the task of inspecting, charging, trying, and sentencing members to eternal perdition. To the brethren in Rome, the apostle Paul asked, *"Who are you to JUDGE another's servant? To HIS OWN master, he stands or falls. Indeed, he will be made to*

stand, for God is able to make him stand" (Romans 14:4, read *1-13).*

There is much more which could be discussed relative to this subject, but it is sufficient at this point to create an AWARENESS relative to the core objectives of the called-out community (*ekklesia*). It will help us understand the **E's** mission of the church later in our studies. It forms a foundation for **back to basics.**

FOR THOUGHT AND DISCUSSION

1. What were your basic beliefs and concepts relative to understanding the English word CHURCH when you became a Christian?

2. In your opinion why is there so much misunderstanding about the word church and how it is used today?

3. How do the words "community" and "assembly" help one understand the nature of the church as described by God?

4. How are sinners "called out" to become part of the "new spiritual community"?

5. How do "clicks" diminish an understanding of the community?

6. How does the word "family" enhance the spiritual community?

7. How is the world influencing understanding, the nature, and practices of the *ekklesia* today?

8. How will you intentionally use this lesson?

UNDERSTANDING THE MISSION OF THE CHURCH

Here are the top and bottom-line questions: **Does each member of your congregation KNOW and PARTICIPATE in the mission of the church as presented in SCRIPTURE?** [ ] Yes [ ] No [ ] Not sure. And the next question is: **How do you know the answer you gave is correct?**

Choose any objective in any field and try to sell it or get participants without going through the following basic "sales sequence":

FIRST, how can anyone know, accept, and do anything he/she is not **aware** of what the objective, need, or benefits? Therefore, time must be spent on creating awareness. In our case, it is an awareness of the mission of the Lord's church. EVERY member must be aware of the **E's** involved in glorifying God (Ephesians 3:21).

SECOND, once I am aware of the objective (the overall mission of the church), do I **understand** it? Understanding is more than a vague awareness, it includes the reasons, values, and intention of the objectives and my participation in them. This is why classroom study is essential and important.

THIRD, once I understand the mission the next question I must answer is do I **believe** it? There is a tendency to know and understand something, and in this case the mission of the church, without believing it applies to me—that I must participate in it.

FOURTH, once I have successfully affirmed my awareness, understanding, and belief in the mission; am I committed to it? The next question is **will I intentionally become actively involved—be a DOER?**

FIFTH, as the mission is being successfully pursued, the next need is an answer to this question: Do **adjustments** or **changes** need to be made in order for the mission to stay on target? In most congregations, the answer is YES. This leads to the next step.

SIXTH, regardless of the answer to number five, an **evaluation** is essential to keeping the program alive, on target, and successful. This will require a specific allotment of time, manpower, and a plan to achieve this objective.

SEVENTH, never take for granted theses six steps. You must **continually** keep the congregation aware and trained in them. The tendency in some congregation is to start and continue a program for a while and then, for various reasons, slowly discontinue it or quickly replace it with a perceived better model. In some cases, the leaders who were for the original program no longer exist or if they do no longer support the program. The mission of the church is **ETERNAL!** We may change or adjust our mode of fulfilling it but we must never change or reduce our emphasis on fulfilling it.

I encourage you to spend some quality time studying this introduction; it sets the tone for the rest of the study.

1. Share with the class, or think about, your personal awareness of the mission of the church.

2. From your awareness what has been the major emphasis given as the mission of the church? Is there one thing? What?

3. If you were assigned the task of creating an awareness campaign relative to the mission of the church how would you do it? Share a tentative plan or approach.

4. What do you perceive as some of the larger challenges you'd face in developing an **E's** awareness program in your church?

5. What additional observations do you have? Be specific.

6. How will you intentionally apply this lesson to your life and ministry? Share your plan. Discuss it.

Lesson 4

WHAT DOES "BACK TO BASICS" MEAN?

An NFL winning coach stands before his players in the first meeting of the new season, holding a football, he says, "Gentleman, this is a football. I don't care how long you've been playing or awards you have, we will begin our season, as we always have, by getting back to the basics; they are the foundation for all the unique calls, special plays, and formations we'll use to win our games. This is a football. Does everyone understand?"

A math teacher stands in front of the freshman class and says, "Ladies and gentlemen we will spend time in our first few weeks going over the fundamentals of Mathematics...yes we will start with 2+2 equals 4."

The Hebrews writer had to remind Christians that they needed to go back to the "first principles"—the basics of the Gospel—which saved them and placed them in the church to become involved in ministry, such as teaching (Cf. Hebrews 5:12; James 3:1, 2).

What does the idiom *Back to Basics* mean? How is it frequently and popularly used today? _Back-to-basics (Adj.)_ means: *"The stressing of simplicity and adherence to basic or fundamental principles. It is advocating a basic approach to prevent or reduce complication, neglect, and none-productive activities related to the major mission and objectives as defined by the company's reasons for existing, etc."*

Back to Basics is also advocated when there is too much concern, too many theories, and activities given to details designed to incorporate what is popular, a new fad, or gimmick. Through proper re-studying, reminders, and return to basics the original mission can once again become the priority. It's easy to see that there is also an application to churches who have moved beyond the basics; thus, they need to return to the "first principles."

What Back To Basics Is Not

Let's take a few minutes and note what the back to basics we are discussing in the study IS NOT:

1. It is not going back and restoring the spirit and practice of dogmatic legalism such as practiced by the Pharisees, scribes, and Sadducees (Read Matthew 23).

2. While we may study and learn from it, back to basics is not trying to model or restore the culture of the First Century.

3. The same may be said of the religious "traditions and practices" (Without book, chapter, and verse) passed on to us by our families). It's not the "We've always done it this way."

4. It is not simply going back no farther than the roots of the "Restoration Movement" (Again only what is contextually true from the Scriptures properly interpreted and applied).

5. It is not trying to hold on to, or go back to, the traditions and rules established by church leaders in past decades or even centuries (Cf. Mark 7:7, 9).

6. It is not an attempt to revive a program from the "good old days" of the church's history. Yes, we may learn but we're not talking about those basics as the end result of our return to basics.

7. Back to basics is not an effort to re-establish the ease, comfort, and control maintained in the "good old days."

I'm not trying to pass judgment on anything you may interpret as a need to go back to, which you refer to as the basics. I'm TOTALLY stressing back to the Scriptures as we see them unfolding in the first years of the church in the First Century.

In summary, biblically speaking, **Back to Basics** places an emphasis on some of the following principles:

1. A return to the previously held values, behaviors, and actions as outlined in Scripture (Cf. 2 Timothy 3:15-17).

2. A return to studying the fundamentals which created the foundation the church is built upon (1 Cor. 3:9-14).

3. A return to exercising the same power—the Gospel—used in the 1st Century to reach the lost (Mark 16:15, 16; Romans 1:14-16).

4. A return to studying, understanding, and applying today the principles and truths used by Christ and His apostles to grow the church for her mission in the world.

5. A return to studying the nature of the *ekklesia* and God's design for it to be a "called out community" of pilgrims and strangers (1 Peter 2:11, 13; Matthew 16:13-19).

6. To slowly, prayerfully, and biblically return the church in the 21st Century to being salt, leaven, light, and a city on a hill—to bring God glory in the church (Ephesians 3:21).

7. A return to studying and applying the truths and principles illustrated in the Book of Acts, Epistles, etc.; recognizing the power and place of local autonomy and shepherds leading the flock (Each of the 7 Churches of Asia were self-governed).

WHY CONGREGATIONS NEED TO GO BACK TO BASICS

There are a number of reasons for getting back to basics. Some are commonsense, some Scriptural, and some are expediencies—all designed to GLORIFY GOD, equip, edify, and evangelize (Plus more).

Some specific reasons may be:

1. The declining membership and lack of new converts.

2. The Gospel isn't being shared with the lost—locally or globally.

3. Lack of interest and participation in programs and activities.

4. Innovations are replacing biblically approved activities.

5. There is a steady decline in zeal and enthusiasm for work.

6. The difficulty in getting teachers and helpers.

7. The decline in all areas of stewardship; especially financial.

8. Difficulty in appointing elders, deacons, preachers, and others for leadership roles.

9. Drifting from the 1st-Century practices which grew churches.

10. Unresolved issues, problems, and sins in congregations.

11. The slow, or fast, inroads of innovations, worldliness, liberalism, and modernism.

12. A lack of self-discipline by members and lack of church discipline of those who "walk disorderly."

13. A failure to identify problems, solutions, and the implementation of solutions—results of effort not identified.

14. A rapid decrease in biblical knowledge, "defending the faith" (Jude 3), and "speaking the truth in love", regardless (Ephesians 4:15).

15. A failure to remember and practice God's BASICS, which are contained within the New Covenant which Jesus died to make a reality (Cf. Matthew 26:28; the book of Hebrews).

All members of the Body of Christ need to know where to GO BACK TO—to know where the BASICS ARE—ALL, from the babe in Christ to the most aged.

FOR THOUGHT AND DISCUSSION

1. In your opinion what are some additional reasons why the church needs to get back to basics?

____

____

____

2. Do you agree with this statement: "The local church will not be
    all God desires it to be without going back to basics?" [ ] Yes
    [ ] No

3. In your opinion what is the number one thing the church—your
    congregation—needs to return to doing as a basic belief or
    practice once again? Why?

4. Take a moment and read chapters 1 through 3 of Revelation.
    What where some of the basics they were failing to heed?

5. If you were going to start a "Back to Basics" effort where would
    you start? Why?

6. What additional observations or questions do you have about
    this lesson?

7. How will you intentionally use this lesson in your life and min-
    istry?

MISUNDERSTANDING OUR BASIC MISSION

Here's a basic truth that is relevant to our study: **We are right where we are, as a rule, because it's where our beliefs and leaders have brought us.** And our beliefs are based on what we have been taught, experienced, believed, decided, and thought.

In Columbus's day, it was believed that the earth was flat; thus all shipping missions were limited by this belief—if you sailed far enough you would fall off the edge of the earth. Fear created a boundary.

A high schooler was hired as a cook and counter person in a fast-food restaurant. When the manager started receiving complaints about the rudeness of the worker, he confronted him. When the boy responded with, "Well, I'm doing my job—taking orders, cooking sometimes—isn't that what you hired me to do?" the manager responded, "NO! I hired you to make my customers happy—that's your mission."

Does every member of a local congregation know what the mission of the church is? Ask a hundred church members if they know the **E's** mission and you'll receive several different answers; ask the same questions of leaders and you'll also get varied answers. Why would this possibly be true?

Let's make the question more specific by asking:

- ✓ How many of you have been in special classes where you studied the biblical mission of the church?
- ✓ Have you heard several sermon series on the mission of the church?
- ✓ Read several articles or books on the mission of the church?
- ✓ Attended seminars or workshops on the mission of the church?
- ✓ Been in discussion groups on the mission of the church?
- ✓ Have you had questions about the mission of the church?
- ✓ Prayed specifically about, and for, the mission of the church?

VARIOUS BELIEFS ABOUT THE MISSION OF THE CHURCH

From research, asking questions, observations, and personal inquiries I have documented a number of beliefs, perceptions, and practices relative to what people in various churches believe about the mission of the church. Here are some of those beliefs as well as various approaches to the mission of the church:

1. Some approach the mission from a theological perspective—what has been deducted in historical studies based on theological beliefs based on dogma, creeds, and Scripture, in most cases, out of context. Thus, the "theology of church missions."

2. Some approach the mission of the church on the basis of long-held traditions handed down from generation to generation. A

popular edification statement of this approach is "We've always done it this way."

3. There are churches which approach the church's mission from their creed, which has been decided by a board, council, etc.

4. Some seek to define and implement the mission of the church based on the needs of society, culture, and relevancy. Thus, it is always in a state of flux.

5. Some approach the mission of the church based on what the "majority" of the member's desire or what is based on what some "missionary" has taught them.

6. Some churches define their mission as being committed to becoming a megachurch, such as seen on TV, i.e. the health, wealth, and social gospel.

7. Some churches see their mission as perpetuating certain biblical doctrines such as keeping the Sabbath, speaking in tongues, the thousand-year reign, etc.

8. Some churches see their mission has specific outreach into poor countries by providing benevolence, etc.

9. Some churches see their mission as being educational—training preachers, teachers, publishing literature, etc.

10. Some churches see their mission as providing a sanctuary where popular and meaningful worship services create a warm and fuzzy feeling; created by musical performances, etc.

11. Some churches see their mission as being cultic by creating communes, isolation of members, and practicing polygamy.

12. There are some churches that exist to promote the strange doctrines, beliefs, and emphasis of the "man of God" who has led them to meet in a storefront.

FOR THOUGHT AND DISCUSSION

1. From your observation and experience what are some of the missions you have seen churches engaged in or emphasizing?

____

____

____

2. In your opinion why are there so many different missions created by so many different churches?_______________________

____

____

3. In your opinion what has influenced your congregation the most in creating your present mission?_______________________

____

____

4. In your opinion why is it important for every member of the church to understand the mission of the church?_______________

____

____

5. Do you understand the mission of the church? [ ] Yes [ ] No

6. What additional observations do you have?

7. How do you plan to intentionally use this lesson? Be specific.

Lesson 6

THE POWER OF KNOWING OUR MISSION

What if President John F. Kennedy had said back on May 25, 1961, "We are going, at some future date, send a man, not sure who it will be, into space to see what's out there…" what would have resulted from that nebulous promise to Congress and the American people?

What's the message in these quotes?

- ✓ *"If you don't know where you are going you might wind up someplace else" (Yogi Bera, baseball manager).*
- ✓ *"If you don't know where you are going, any road will get you there" (Lewis Carrol, Alice in Wonderland).*
- ✓ *"If you don't know where you are going any old road will do." (Unknown).*
- ✓ *"There's a road which seems right but the end thereof is the way of destruction" (King Solomon).*

The message I get from these quotes is that a life lived without purpose, goals, and a mission achieves very little or nothing at all. What do you think? **There is power in knowing the mission!**

The message I also get is that a congregation moving from day to day, month to month, and year to year without specific purpose, goals, and mission is falling short of what God desires. Only planning from one service to another is not fulfilling the mission Christ has given His church, which is His body (Colossians 1:18)

Think about the 12 ragtag unknown blue-collar workers, with only a synagogue education, and no leadership or management experience chosen by Jesus to be students in his school of discipling. Thinking about this reminds me of what Gandhi said: *A small body of determined spirits fired by an unquenchable faith in the mission can alter the course of human history*." This was certainly true of those chosen by Christ and given, along with Paul, the mission of the church. A mission which is expressed in what I choose to call the preliminary and core, combined, **12-E's mission.** These are:

1. **Erosion of Spiritual Values**
2. **Enthusiasm for the Mission**
3. **Exploring Scripture**
4. **Enthroning God**
5. **Exalting Christ**
6. **Equipping Members**
7. **Edifying Members**
8. **Evangelizing the Lost**
9. **Explosive Church Growth & Conversions**
10. **Endeavoring to Maintain Unity**
11. **Engaging the enemy--Satan**
12. **Enduring through Faith**

These **12-E's** will be developed in the lessons which follow. This study is really **Back to Basics.** The order of study is your choice.

From time to time we hear or even engage in actions referred to by these three words—**Back to Basics.** They are spoken with reference to sports teams, businesses, and companies, organizations of every type; even churches.

The principle of **Back to Basics** is referred to by the Hebrews writer: *"For though by this time you OUGHT to be TEACHERS, you NEED someone to teach you AGAIN the FIRST principles of the oracles of God, and you have need milk and not solid food"* (Hebrews 5:12; Cf. 13-6:3).

The church's overall mission is summarized in one Ephesians 3:21. **To glorify God:** *"[T]o Him be GLORY in the CHURCH by Christ Jesus to all generations, forever and ever. Amen."* In Romans 11:36, *"For of Him and through Him, and to Him are ALL THINGS, to whom be GLORY forever. Amen."*

The core mission to glorify God the Father and Jesus Christ contains powerful and essential parts of the **12-E's.** It isn't a rare or forced thing to have a single mission statement that is supported and fulfilled by various goals and actions.

As a veteran of the U.S. Navy, I was, and am, keenly aware of the mission which follows: *"The mission of the **NAVY** is to maintain, Train, equip combat-ready naval forces capable of winning wars, deterring* *aggression and maintain freedom of the seas."(www.Navy.com). Notice the mission has 6 parts: (1) maintain, (2) train, (3) equip, (4) win wars, (5) deterring aggression, and (6) maintain freedom of the seas.*

As soldiers of Christ we must be aware of, understand, and carry out our mission which has **12-E's.** Here is a review of our mission as soldiers: *"You, therefore, must ENDURE hardship as a good SOLDIER of Jesus Christ. No one engaged in warfare entangles himself with the affairs of this life, that he may please him who enlisted him as a soldier"* *(2 Timothy 2:3, 4).*

When a person is converted and added to the body (church) by God (1 Corinthians 12:18), he becomes a new member of God's mission team. In time he/she will develop into an active and contributing member of the **12-E's** mission (Cf. Hebrews 4:12, 13). As each member functions in their role in their mission, as the Bible teaches, the church moves forward In GLORIFYING GOD.

FOR THOUGHT AND DISCUSSION

1. How balanced would you say your congregation is in placing an emphasis on the 12-Es with frequency? [ ] Excellent [ ] Good [ ] Okay [ ] Rare [ ] Not at all [ ] Other:_____________

2. How aware would you say the "average member" is of the mission of the church? [ ] Very [ ] Average [ ] Fair [ ] None

3. Why do you suppose some congregations place an emphasis on only one of the **12-E's**—Evangelism?

____

____

____

4. Why, if it is, important that we go **Back to Basics**?

____

____

____

5. How motivated are you about studying the **12-E's** mission of the local church? [ ] Excellent [ ] Very [ ] Okay [ ] Not at all.

6. What additional observations do you have?

7. How do you plan to intentionally use this lesson?

Lesson 7

THINKING BIBLICALLY ABOUT OUR MISSION

Have you ever been on a mission trip? [ ] Yes [ ] No. To me the word mission is an exciting word; whether in spiritual matters or what we refer to as secular matters. To have a goal, plan, and action steps that you carry out for reaching it by keeping life active and exciting.

From typing in "what is the mission of the church?' on Goggle there evidently is a lot of interest in this question. There were 476,000,000 inquiries. Spending a few minutes reading some of the answers it is obvious there is a lot of interest, answers, ignorance, and misunderstanding relative to the mission of the church. Here are some of the answers.

1. *Set the right Mission Statement for your church.*
2. *Properly define the mission of your church.*
3. *What, really, is the mission of the local church?*
4. *Why be concerned with a mission statement for a church?*
5. *Who is responsible for setting the church's mission statement?*
6. *How do Christians set a mission statement for their church?*
7. *When does a church need a mission statement?*
8. *The church's mission statement should be tied to its vision.*
9. *The mission of the church is to meet community needs.*

10. *The mission of the church changes from generation to generation, society to society, and culture to culture. It is always in a state of flux.*

These 10 are only a drop in the bucket compared to the almost unending statements relative to answering "What is the mission of the church?" Seems like everyone has an answer or opinion.

JESUS AND OUR UNDERSTANDING OF MISSION

The Christian understands, whether he practices it or not, that involved in mission is going and doing something near or far. It may be in a congregational facility or in a distant place or facility.

Question: What is the longest mission trip someone has ever gone on? Where and by whom? My longest is a 17-hour flight to New Zealand from Denver via LAX airport. How about your trip?

The record for the longest missionary trip documented in history is held by Jesus Christ. It was when He left eternity and the "heavens of the heavens" to travel to earth and be lodged in the womb of a virgin for 9 months and then make his way out of the birth canal to be born in a little remove place on the map called Nazareth. He whom the heaven of heavens couldn't contain was housed for 30-plus years in a coat of flesh and blood. He came on a mission which He fulfilled.

The Incarnate Son of God announced His mission numerous times during His brief stay on earth:

1. **Luke 19:10,** "[F]or the Son of man has come to seek and save that which was lost."

2. **Matthew 26:28,** *"For this is My blood of the new covenant, which is shed for many for the remission of sins."*

3. **John 10:10,** *"The thief does not come except to steal, and to kill, and to destroy. I have come that they may have life and have it more abundantly."*

4. **John 11:25,** *"Jesus said to her, 'I am the resurrection and the life, He who believes in Me, though he may die, he shall live."*

5. **John 12:46,** *I have come as a light into the world, that whoever believes in Me should not abide in darkness."*

6. **Mark 1:38,** *"But He said to them, 'Let us go into the next towns, that I may preach there also because for this purpose I have come forth."*

7. **John 4:25, 26,** *"The woman said to Him, 'I know the Messiah is coming' (who is called Christ). 'When He comes, He will tell us all things.' Jesus said to her, 'I who speaks to you am He'".*

John the Baptist made this observation about the mission of Jesus, *"The next day John saw Jesus coming toward him, and said, 'Behold! The Lamb of God who takes away the sin of the world"* (John 1:29).

At His birth it was announced, *"And she will bring forth a Son, and you shall call his name Jesus, for he will save His people from their sins"* (Matthew 1:21).

When Jesus was 12-years-old He announced clearly what His mission in life was. Speaking to his parents, He said: *"... Why did you seek*

Me? Did you not know that I must be about My Father's business?" *(Luke 2:49).* What were our aspirations at 12?

Dying on the cross Jesus announced that He had finished His mission (John 19:30). After His resurrection which proved He was the Son of God with power; He announced His possession of ALL AUTHORITY in heaven and on earth; giving His disciples a global mission to preach the Gospel by making disciples all over the world. (Matthew 29:18-20).

Before His ascension to heaven Jesus gave His final orders relative to the sequence in geography they would follow in carrying out the evangelism mission: *"But you shall receive power when the Holy Spirit has come upon you; and you shall be witnesses to Me in Jerusalem, and in Judea and Samaria, and to the ends of the earth"* *(Acts 1:8).*

THE CHRISTIAN LIFE AND MISSION

I AFFIRM: the daily Christian life is one of being on a perpetual mission for and with our Lord and Savior Jesus Christ. As the hymn affirms, *"Where He leads me I will follow."*

The Christian's life mission centers in glorifying God—Ephesians 3:21—and pursuing the **12-E's** components tied to making the ultimate mission a reality. In order to succeed in this amazing and honorable mission we must have several qualities:

First, we must have the **attitude of Christ:** *"Your attitude should be the same as that of Christ Jesus… He humbled Himself and became obedient to death, even the death of the cross…"* *(Philippians 2:5-8).*

Second, we must pursue our mission by **walking by faith:** *"For we walk by faith, not by sight. We are confident, yes, well pleased rather be absent from the body and to be well-pleasing to the Lord"* (2 Corinthians 5:7, 8).

Third, we must be **zealous unto every good work.** "[W]ho gave Himself for us, that He might redeem us from every lawless deed and purify for Himself His own special people, ZEALOUS FOR GOOD WORKS" (Titus 2:14).

Fourth, we must **abide in Christ and bear much fruit.** *"By this, My Father is glorified, that you bear much fruit; so you will be my disciple. As the Father loved Me, I also have loved you; abide in My love"* (John 15:8, 9). This includes the *"fruit of the Spirit"* (Galatians 5:22-26).

Fifth, once we put our hands to the plow **we must not look back:** *"But Jesus said to him, 'No one, having put his hand to the plow, and looking back, is fit for the kingdom of God"* (Luke 9:62). *"Forgetting those things which are behind, I press on to the goal"* (Apostle Paul).

Sixth, we must **keep our minds set on things, not on things below, but things above:** *"If then you were raised with Christ, seek those things which are ABOVE, where Christ is, and sitting at the right hand of God. SET your MIND on things above, not on things on the earth"* (Colossians 3:1- 2).

Seventh, we must **contend for the faith.** *"Beloved, while I was very diligent to write to you concerning our common salvation, I found it* *necessary to write to you exhorting you to CONTEND EARNESTLY for the faith which was once for all delivered to the saints"* (Jude 1:3).

These 7 must qualities are merely examples of the many we can find in the pages of Scripture. We must BE and DO the qualities God desires in our daily lives. And by so doing we are fulfilling part of our mission as light, salt, leaven, and city on a hill which will draw people to the Gospel (Cf. Romans 1:14-16).

FOR THOUGHT AND DISCUSSION

1. What comes to mind when the words "Mission Statement" is heard or used?
2. Does your job or business have a mission statement?
3. How has the church been influenced, either in a positive or negative way, by adopting the world's approach to developing a mission statement?
4. Why is it important for the church to understand Jesus' personal mission statements?
5. Do you have a personal mission statement? Share it.
6. What additional qualities would you add to those mentioned?
7. What additional thoughts do you have about this lesson?
8. How will you intentionally use this lesson in your life and ministry?

Part 2

The Preliminary Basics

[The First 3-E's of the 12]

EROSION OF SPIRITUAL VALUES

A while back I had to have a new water line run from the street to my house because of a leak. The plumbers dug up the ground laying and installing the pipe. However, they didn't replace the grass. The ground was left bare. I kept saying I was going to get the areas re-sodded but one excuse after another prevented me. Then one day after a big Georgia rain I was walking along the fence where the pipe had been laid and noticed a major case of erosion was starting to occur. A deep rut, loose rocks, and eroded soil were evident. I finally woke up.

EROSION! In earth science erosion is the action of surface processes that remove soil, rock, dead grass, or dissolved materials from the location of the Earth's crust, and then transported to another location (*Wikipedia*).

Science has invented a "control blanket or mat", which you've no doubt seen on highway banks and yards of new houses. They cover erosion areas—holding the seed, mulches, and soil in place until vegetation is established.

EROSION is also used to describe values—VALUE EROSION." It refers to a segment of society, where a particular VALUE is substantially realized, its status can be ERODED, the value loses its attractiveness" and comes to be downgraded by disenchantment and disillusion-ment" (*encyclopedia.uia.org*).

The *Social Science Journal* lists 34 erosions of values (Sept 2016, pp 34, 35). Here are some of the broad categories: (1) Erosion in social values, (2) Cultural values, (3) Economical values, (4) Political values, etc. These all have numerous sub-sets. What was obviously missing was the erosion of SPIRITUAL VALUES. Which to me is one of the major causes, if not the major cause, of erosion in all the identified areas.

SPIRITUAL EROSION IN THE CHURCH

The local congregation of God's people—the church—has from the very beginning been challenged by erosion. It is because of the various forms erosion takes and the damages it causes, that it is the first **E** in our list of preliminary **E's**. It is because of evident erosion occurring in our mission as a church that we MUST return to the BASICS. In section one of our study, we had a brief look at fundamentals related to the Lord's called out body—the *ekklesia*—church.

Here is a quick reminder of some central facts we need to remember about Jesus' church:

1. Jesus is the only builder (Matthew 16:17-20).
2. Jesus is the only foundation (1 Corinthians 3:9-15).
3. Jesus is the only head (Colossians 1:18, 24).
4. He adds the members to the church (Acts 2:47, 1 Cor. 12:18)

5. The church is the Lord's house (1 Timothy 3:15).

6. The church is glorious (Ephesians 5:27).

7. We bring God glory in the church (Eph. 3:21).

Just as the physical Temple in Jerusalem was being abused (John 2:13-17), the body of Christ, though not in the physical sense, can and is being abused or eroded today. Look around! Do you see in the past, present, or possible future erosions impacting the church? [ ] Yes [ ] No.

While we usually are, we shouldn't be surprised when signs of spiritual erosion start to occur. Paul warned the young preacher, Timothy, to be on guard because erosions were coming:

"But know this, that in the last days perilous times will come: For men will be lovers of themselves, lovers of money, boasters, proud, blasphemers, disobedient to parents, unthankful, unholy, unloving, unforgiving, slanders, without self-control, brutal, despisers of good, traitors, headstrong, haughty, lover of pleasure rather than lovers of God, having a form of godliness but denying its power: And from such turn away" (2 Timothy 3:1-5).

Paul covered both the world and the church; in both spheres, there would be an erosion of the core spiritual values.

In another warning in the same book, just a few verses away Paul warned Timothy again about what was up ahead as he preached:

We can see erosions starting to occur in some of the churches mentioned in the Scriptures. Five of the Seven Churches of Asia were in states of erosion (Cf. Revelation 2 & 3). The church in Corinth was riddled with numerous evidence of erosion, both doctrinally about the resurrection (Chapter 15), and personally about going to court (1 Corinthians 6:1-6); there was even an incest situation (1 Corinthians 5:1-12). (Read 1 Corinthians for the complete picture of erosion)

The Scriptures document, in some cases by name, those who were guilty of erosive behavior and attitudes:

1. Ananias and his wife, Sapphira, lied to the church about how they handled the proceeds from the sale of the property. They died on the spot (Acts 5:1-11).

2. Paul wrote this about one of his fellow-workers: *'[F]or Demas has forsaken me, having loved this present world, and departed*

for Thessalonica—Crescens for Galatia. Titus for Dalmatia" (2 Timothy" (2 Timothy 4:10).

3. The apostle John calls by name a member of the church who had taken upon himself the authority to be the gatekeeper of the flock:

> *"I wrote to the CHURCH, but Diotrephes, who loves to have the PREEMINENCE among them, does not receive us. Therefore, if I come, I will call to mind his deeds which he does, prating against us with malicious words. And not content with that, he himself does not receive the brethren, and forbids those who wish to, putting them out of the church" (3 John 9, 10).*

Solomon was right, there is nothing new under the sun... just a new bunch digging up old practices and sins. "A rose by any other names smells the same." This is why we MUST, if we care about the present and future of the church, get BACK TO BASICS.

POSSIBLE SIGNS OF EROSION TODAY

Just as the Old Testament was written and preserved for our learning (Romans 15:4); the New Testament serves the same purpose. *"We have been given all things which pertain to life and godliness (2 Peter 1:3).*

Jesus gave us a God-approved litmus test by which we can notice and identify signs of erosion: *"Beware of false prophets, who come to you in sheep's clothing, but inwardly they are ravenous wolves. You will KNOW them by their FRUITS. Do men gather grapes from thorn bushes or figs from thistles?"(Matthew 7:15, 16).* Here are some possible fruit indicators—lack of fruit—that the church is facing a number of erosions today:

1. Drifting away from the traditional forms of worship conducted in the assemblies; especially on Sunday. Some of these include instruments of music, females leading prayer, making announcements, and officiating at the Lord's Table.

2. A decline in attendance at the various church activities, and especially the worship services (Hebrews 10:24, 25). In many congregations less than 50% return on Sunday and Wednesday evenings. Some have discontinued Sunday evening services.

3. There is more and more emphasis relative to the "meet my needs" mentality promoted by the carnality of the world's marketing strategy. We need to let God tell us what our needs are.

4. The gradual shift from an emphasis on biblical Christianity to a carnal acceptance of "Churchianity."

5. Presenting health, wealth, and feel-good pop psychology message instead of "preaching the word" (2 Timothy 4:1-5).

6. There seems to be more and more of the world influencing the church instead of the church influencing the world (1 John 5:19; Mark 15:15, 16).

7. A loss of the biblical model of servant leadership by elders, preachers, deacons, teachers, etc. to the CEO business model.

8. A lack of discipline relative to those who sin openly, bring reproach on the Bride of Christ; and quit serving Him as Lord.

9. An emphasis on "tearing down barns" and building "bigger barns" with the hope of attracting the lost as well as increasing their own comfort with brick and mortar.

10. A trend toward a "professional clergy" who is more sophisticated and educated than past generations.

11. A gradual decrease in emphasizing the "whole church family" and fellowship of all believers by dividing or segregating the members into age groups, educational levels, professions, etc.

12. A drifting away from textual studies in Bible classes to feel good, humanistic and psychological needs. There is a growing level of ignorance of the Scriptures "rightly divided" (2 Timothy 2:15).

What possible erosions would you add to this list?

1.____

2.____

The above 12 examples are not accusations against every congregation of the Lord's people; if there's one that's one too many. It's just a wakeup reminder or preventive lesson to help avoid Satan's attempt to destroy the Bride of Christ, inch by inch, drip by drip, drifting slowly without an alarm bell sounding a warning. It's a *"Wake up thou that sleepiest"* principle (Ephesians 5:14).

FOR THOUGHT AND DISCUSSION

1. What experience have you had in dealing with "physical erosion"?

2. What are some signs of erosion taking place in our nation?

3. What are some signs of erosion taking place in the home?

4. From your observations are there any signs of erosion taking place in the Lord's church? If so, what are some of them?

5. How relevant is it to get back to Bible basics to discover, correct, and prevent spiritual erosions?

6. What additional observations do you have?

7. How will you intentionally work on avoiding erosions in your life?

ENTHUSIASM FOR THE MISSION

Before we dig deeper into the amazing study of the **E's** in returning back to basics, we need to take some quality time studying the place and role enthusiasm must play in our gaining the ultimate benefits and blessings from digging deeper.

"Enthusiasm," wrote Ralph Waldo Emerson," *is one of the most powerful engines of success. When you do a thing, do it with your might. Put your whole soul into it. Stamp it with your personality. Be active, be energetic, be enthusiastic and faithful, and you will accomplish your object. Nothing great was ever achieved without enthusiasm."*

What is your definition of enthusiasm?_______________________

____

Who is the most enthusiastic person you know?_______________

____

The Bible has several words that convey being filled with enthusiasm: ardor, zeal, eager, wholeheartedness, passion, etc. The two basic Greek words translated enthusiasm are **_en_** and **_theos_**—with **_theos_** being the Greek word for God; thus in its root concept **_entheos_** *means "full of God; influenced by God; moved by God."*

In John 2:17 we read where Jesus was enthusiastic in dealing with the money changers in the temple; the word ZEAL is used: *"Then His disciples remembered that it was written, 'Zeal for Your house has eaten me up'" (Cf. Psalm 69:9).* Jesus was emotionally under control.

The word zeal is from the Greek word **_zelos_** *which is a form of* **_zeo_** which means *"to boil; to be white-hot."* As a metaphor or figurative meaning it refers to *"fervent; ardent on behalf of someone; noble aspirations; to have a strong affection towards; to be totally devoted."*

Here are some verses where zeal is used:

1. <u>Titus 2:14:</u> *"[W]ho gave Himself for us the He might redeem us from EVERY lawless deed and purify for Himself His own people, ZEALOUS for good works."* Our study of back to the basics will not be successful if we are not ZEALOUS FOR GOOD WORKS! Lukewarmness will not motivate us for very long.

2. <u>Acts 21:20:</u> *"And when they heard it, they glorified the Lord. And they said to* him, 'You see, brother, how many myriads of Jews there are who have believed, and they are all ZEALOUS for the law." Enthusiasm can be redirected as we see in this case of those Jewish converts. It is a personal choice.

3. <u>Galatians 4:17, 18:</u> *"They ZEALOUSLY court you, but for no good; yes, they want to exclude you, that you may be ZEALOUS for them. But it is GOOD to be ZEALOUS in a good thing always,*

and not only when I am present with you." Enthusiasm can be used for ulterior motives; we must be on guard against it.

4. <u>Colossians 4:12, 13:</u> *"Epaphras, who is one of you, a bondservant of Christ, greets you, always laboring FERVENTLY for you in prayer, that you may stand perfect and complete in all the will of God. For I bear him witness that he has a great ZEAL for you, and those who are in Laodicea, and those in Hierapolis."* This is a powerful illustration of how one's Christian's zeal influenced and blessed others.

5. <u>Revelation 3:19:</u> *"As many as I love, I rebuke and chasten. Therefore be ZEALOUS and repent.* This was one of the 7 churches in Asia. It was diagnosed by the Lord as neither being hot or cold—just lukewarm—it needed to turn up the fire of commitment and become "white-hot again"—ZEALOUS—which required repentance.

The missions of the Bride (church) of Christ will not be accomplished by cold, lukewarm, or indifferent members of the body. This is why we must start with ENTHUSIASM.

HANDS TO THE PLOW

Years ago I was then, and still am, impressed with this quote: "A man with enthusiasm and a rusty wrench can accomplish more than a talker of great things with an expensive toolbox will accomplish, he is lazy." Sadly, a lot of time in some congregations is spent talking about, investigating possibilities, and affirming belief in DOING the missions of the church but never getting around to actually doing it. It is the opposite of what James commanded us to *"be DOERS of the word and not just hearers only" (James 1:24-27).*

Jesus used the metaphor of a farmer to warn us about starting right but dying in the middle of our plowing effort: *"But Jesus said to him, 'No one having put his hand to the plow, and looking back, is fit for the kingdom of God" (Luke 9:62).* King Solomon nailed it with these words, *"Better is the ending of thing than the beginning of it" (Eccl. 7:9).*

THE EAGER CHRISTIAN

From time to time we see news accounts of people lining up the day before outside a retail store to buy a new phone that'll go on sale the next day. They are eager to be the first or maybe be assured of getting a new phone. Other events such as sporting or concerts have the same show of eagerness. What if there was an eagerness to attend church?

Eagerness is the product of enthusiasm or may well be just another name for it. Here are some Bible verses which illustrate eagerness among first-century Christians:

1. <u>1 Corinthians 14:2:</u> *"So with yourselves; since you are EAGER for the manifestation of the Spirit, strive to EXCEL in building up the church."* What a needed attitude and action by Christians in the 21st-Century. What if every Christian EXCELLED?

2. <u>1 Peter 5:2</u>: *"Tend the flock of God that is in your charge, not by constraint but willingly, not for shameful gain but EAGERLY."* Imagine an eldership eagerly tending the flock and a flock that wanted to be eagerly tended.

3. <u>2 Corinthians 8:11</u>: *"Now finish the work, so that your EAGER willingness to do it may be matched by your completion of it, according to your means"* (NIV). What would it look like this Sunday if every attendee was EAGER for the collection plate to come to his or her hands? How about attending Wednesday?

4. <u>Titus 2:14:</u> *"Who gave Himself for us to redeem us from all wickedness and to purify for Himself a people that are also His own, EAGER to what is GOOD."* What if every day every Christians went about eagerly trying to do what is good—what would the results be? The world "would see Jesus" in us.

What are some suggestions for helping the church return to the basic power of EAGERNESS, Yes! We must first be EAGER to do so.

Hesitation
Upon the plains of hesitation
Bleached the bones of countless millions
Who on the threshold of victory
Sat down to wait, and waiting died

THE EBB AND FLOW OF ENTHUSIASM

Enthusiasm, zeal, eagerness, and passion are basic emotions created within our hearts. Therefore, they are subject to high and low points.

In his writings, the apostle Paul was not reluctant to talk about his high and low points, his times of being abused and times of being praised. No one can stay on a "pep rally spiritual high." However, we can have a base scale where we will always return to and resume our zeal for the Lord.

The Scriptures include encouraging remarks and commands not to be overcome with evil, frustrations, and weariness:

1. **Galatians 6:9:** *"And let us not grow weary while doing good, for in due season we shall reap if we do not LOSE HEART."* Paul is saying don't give out, give in, or give up—keep on keeping on—the prize is up ahead.

2. **Hebrews 12:3:** *"For consider Him who endured such hostility from sinners against Himself, lest you become weary and discouraged in your souls."* The Scriptures tell it like it is—there is always the danger of losing our zeal; we must keep our eyes on the cross and prize of heaven (John 11:1-7).

3. **2 Thessalonians 3:13:** *"But as for you, brethren, do not grow weary in doing good."* Yes, it's possible to be discouraged when you work and see little or no results; or take two steps forward and one back.

4. **2 Corinthians 11:22-33:** In these verses, the apostle Paul wrote about all the suffering he endured as a faithful servant of

Christ. In verse 27, we read: *"...in WEARINESS and toil, in sleeplessness often, in hunger and thirst, in fasting often, in cold and nakedness..."* Yet, Paul never gave up or lost his enthusiasm for serving the Lord, he *"knew in whom he believed."*

5. **Malachi 2:17:** *You have WEARIED the LORD with your words; yet you say, 'In what way have we WEARIED Him?' In that, you say, 'Everyone who does evil is good in the sight of the LORD, and He delights in them,' or, 'Where is the God of justice?'"* The impatient people were accusing God of favoring the sinners; they failed to see that God works on His own schedule. God was tired of their misunderstandings and accusations.

Remember the dynamic and courageous work of Elijah as he confronted the prophets of Baal (Cf. 1 Kings 18). After the amazing victory, a time when Elijah's enthusiasm should have been at an all-time high, we see his spirit hit rock bottom and he ran away and secluded himself, with a death wish (Cf. 1 Kings 19:4-10).

Yes, we can grow weary in doing what God has commanded. Our birth certificate says we are human, and as such we will have those Elijah moments. But we must recognize what is happening and have a plan to bounce back with more enthusiasm than ever. We must have the attitude of the Psalmist who said, *"Though I walk in the midst of trouble, You will REVIVE me; You will stretch out Your hand against the wrath of my enemies, and Your right hand will save me" (Psalm 138:7).*

KEYS TO BEING ENTHUSIASTIC

Since Scriptures command us to be ZEALOUS and avoid growing WEARY, we must be able to do so—therefore, enthusiasm is a choice. Here are some basic keys for developing and maintaining zeal for the Lord and His work:

1. Every day, moment by moment, remember all the blessings and benefits God is giving you (Cf. Psalm 103:2).
2. Continually focus on how much God loves you, how He is saving you through the blood of Christ (Romans 5:1-10).
3. Remember to make the Lord's Supper every Sunday one of your focal events to rehearse all God has, is, and shall continue to do for you (Matthew 26:26-30; 1 Corinthians 11:23-34).
4. Never forget that your enthusiasm is not tied to the ebb and flow of the Stock Market or any other earthly success. Jesus told His disciples, *"...rejoice because your names are written in heaven" (Luke 10:20).*
5. Never lose your fascination with the basics of Christianity: The life, death, burial, resurrection, ascension, and return of Christ (Cf. 1 Corinthians 16:1-7). There's no way you can lose your zeal if you continually study, meditate, and take action because of a deeper understanding of Christ's victory for you.
6. Never take your eyes off the end goal—Heaven (1 Peter 1:3-11). Living faithfully to the end guarantees the crown.

7. Always be on guard relative to the fact that Satan is continually trying to steal the word out of your heart (Cf. Luke 8:11-15). Therefore, daily work on bringing forth mature fruit (Luke 8:15; John 15:1-8).

FOR THOUGHT AND DISCUSSION

1. How does enthusiasm relate to the mission of the church?

2. What are some robbers of zeal for the Lord's work?

3. How is enthusiasm misunderstood? Why?

4. What are some ways to revive lost enthusiasm?

5. Discuss Paul's zeal in spite of his sufferings?

6. Discuss Elijah's loss of enthusiasm.

7. What additional observations do you have?

8. How will you intentionally improve and demonstrate your zeal?

E-3

EXPLORING THE SCRIPTURE

What a scene! A leader from Ethiopia, a eunuch in charge of Queen Candice's treasure, is riding along in a bouncing chariot, not taking in the scenery of the desert but reading the expensive scroll of Isaiah, a major prophet in Israel's history. Out of the blue, his concentration is interrupted by a man running alongside his chariot. The runner shouts a question, "Do you understand what you are reading?" The eunuch was reading Isaiah 53. Who was this interrupter?

The eunuch could have responded that it was none of Philip's, as an intruder, business (Read Acts 8:26-31). Instead, he responded, "How can I, unless someone GUIDES me?" His heart was open and honest. There was something very compelling about Isaiah 53 (Stop and go read it). The eunuch wanted to understand what he was reading (Which should be the attitude of every reader).

In this historical portion of Scripture, we have the first account of an evangelist out on a road stopping a lost person and sharing the Gospel and baptizing him into Christ (Acts 8:35-39). It is one thing, a commendable thing, to have a (1) copy of the Scripture (Bible), (2) have the ability to read it, (3), yet another challenge to understand without (4) someone explaining the Scriptures. This is why our next **lesson** in the preliminary **Back to Basics** is **Exploring the Scriptures.** All the E's are built on the foundation of Scripture which must be understood.

BIBLICAL EMPHASIS ON EXPLORING THE SCRIPTURE

Let's take a moment and define EXPLORE. It basically means, *"To look into closely; examine thoroughly; investigate; to probe; to learn about; search out"*, etc.

The core of our relationship with God and being committed to faithfully DOING His word depends on (1) knowing the word, (2) understanding the word, and (3) doing the word (Cf. James 1:22-27). This is the starting point: WE MUST EXPLORE THE SCRIPTURE. Here are some key Scriptures relevant to this point.

1. <u>Matthew 22:29</u>: *"Jesus answered and said to them, 'You are mistaken, not knowing the Scriptures nor the power of God."*

2. <u>Mark 12:10</u>: *"Have you not read this Scripture…?"*

3. <u>Luke 24:27</u>: "And beginning at Moses and all the Prophets, He EXPOUNDED to them in ALL the Scriptures the things concerning Himself."

4. <u>John 5:39</u>: "You SEARCH the Scriptures for in them you think you have eternal life, and these are they which testify of me."

5. <u>John 7:52</u>: "They answered and said to him, 'Are you also from Galilee? SEARCH and look, for no prophet has arisen out of Galilee.'"

6. <u>John 10:35:</u> "If He called them gods, to whom the word of God came (and the Scripture cannot be broken)."

7. <u>Acts 1:16:</u> "Men and brethren, this Scripture had to be fulfilled, which the Holy Spirit spoke before by the mouth of David concerning Judas, who became a guide to those who arrested Jesus."

8. <u>Acts 17:2:</u> "Then Paul, as his custom was, went in to them, and for three Sabbaths reasoned with them from SCRIPTURES."

9. <u>Acts 17:11:</u> "These (i.e. Jews) were more fair-minded than those in Thessalonica, in that they received the word with all readiness, and SEARCHED the Scriptures daily to find out whether these things were so."

10. <u>Romans 4:3:</u> "For what does the Scripture say? *'Abraham believed God, and it was accounted to him for righteousness.*"

THE UNIQUENESS OF SCRIPTURES

The Holy Bible is unique for a number of reasons:

1. It contains 66 books divided into two major divisions: The Old and New Testaments.

2. It was written over a period of approximately 4000 years by 40 different men who were not all in contact with each other; in most cases separated by centuries.

3. The core theme of the Bible related to 3 truths: (1) Someone is coming—Jesus, (2) Someone has come—Jesus, and (3) Someone is coming again—Jesus.

4. The Scriptures are "God-breathed" (2 Timothy 3:15-17).

5. The Canon of Scripture (unity of the 66 books rightly divided) made it possible for all who desire to do the same thing—thus uniformity and unity. The word "Canon" is a Greek word that refers to "A straight rod or bar to determine other things. It is a guide or a model to follow; it serves as a standard to regulate. It is used as a figure or metaphor several times in the New Testament:

   (a) <u>Galatians 6:16:</u> *"As many as walk according to this rule, peace be on them..."*

   (b) <u>Philippians 3:16:</u> *"... Let us walk by the same rule..."*

   (c) <u>2 Corinthians 10:13:</u> *"... According to the measure of the rule which God hath distributed to us ..."*

   (d) <u>2 Corinthians 10:15:</u> *"... Be enlarged by you according to our rule..."*

6. It's because of the Canon of Scriptures that we are able to establish and maintain the Unity of the Spirit (Ephesians 4:1-7).

7. The Scriptures, not the rules, programs, and traditions of men, will be the standard by which we will be judged in the end (Hebrews 9:27; John 12:48, 49).

Through the centuries men have tried to destroy the Bible. Voltaire said, "Another century and there will not be a Bible on earth." The years have come and gone since his statement; the Bible still remains the bestseller and most circulated book. It is translated into more languages than any other book.

AUTHORITY AND SCRIPTURE

Why we do things is important in every area of life; especially when it comes to our relationship with God and with one another in the church. On one occasion Jesus was challenged relative to the authority question:

Matthew 21:23, 24: *Now when He came into the temple, the chief priests and the elders of the people CONFRONTED Him as He was TEACHING, and said, 'By what AUTHORITY are You doing these things? And who gave you this authority?' But Jesus answered and said to them, 'I also will ask you one thing, which if you tell Me, I likewise will tell you by what AUTHORITY I do these things.'"*

Even though the Jewish leaders were trying to trap Jesus or find reasons to discredit Him, in the right context there two questions have validity:

1. *"By what AUTHORITY are You doing these things?"*
2. *"And who gave you this authority?"*

Today the church is challenged as perhaps never before over the issue of authority. Sadly, in some congregations, the rules, habits, traditions, and expediencies created by Christians set aside the "commandments of God." The "margin of a vote" or the usurping of authority is the WHY and WHO is behind the "authority."

What is AUTHORITY"? It is the Greek word _exousia_ and means to _"have a privilege, right, or granting the right, etc."_ For example, the Hebrews' writer had this in mind when he wrote this about Jesus and His authority. "[T]_hough He was a Son, yet he learned OBEDIENCE by the things which He suffered. And having been perfected, He became the AUTHOR of eternal salvation to all who OBEY HIM"_ (Hebrews 5:8, 9).

After His resurrection from the dead, Jesus was given ALL AUTHORITY in heaven and earth:

Matthew 28:18-20: _"And Jesus came and spoke to them, saying, 'ALL AUTHORITY has been given to Me in heaven and on earth. Go therefore and make disciples of all nations, baptizing them in the name of the Father and of the Son and of the Holy Spirit, teaching them to OBSERVE all the things I have COMMANDED, you, and lo, I am with you always, even to the end of the age.' Amen."_

The authority of Christ is vested in His word which will judge us (John 12:48), as well as what His disciples/Apostles taught:

1. **Mark 1:22:** *"And they were astonished at His teaching, for He taught them as one having AUTHORITY, and not as the scribes."*

2. **Luke 9:1, 2:** *"Then He called His twelve disciples together and gave them power and AUTHORITY over all demons, and to cure diseases. He sent them to PREACH the kingdom of God and to heal the sick."*

3. **Titus 2:15:** *"Speak these things, exhort, and rebuke with all AUTHORITY. Let no one despise you."*

4. **1 Timothy 2:12:** *"And I do not permit a woman to teach or to have AUTHORITY over a man, but to be in silence."*

BACK TO EXPLORING SCRIPTURE TODAY

The challenges we face today are not much different than they were in the First Century; just more people, new names for sin and greater effort to invent evil:

1. The Jews were divided into numerous groups which believed each was the right one to usher in the age of the Messiah. The church is divided today over opinions, traditions, personalities, doctrines, facilities, and more.

2. The world of the First Century was a cauldron of political unrest with various groups trying to wrest and hold power; much like the world of our day in Washington, D.C. and locally.

3. The world of the First Century was filled with paganism, cultic religions, immorality in unspeakable forms, much like in our day except we are outdoing them through our media.

4. The world of the First Century was filled with violence, prejudice, crime, wars, and rumors of war, much like in the USA.

5. The world of the First Century was in the throes of philosophical speculations; limited education for the elite; servitude and low wages; language barriers, much like it is in our country today.

6. Then, as now, people were inventors of every kind of evil.

These six observations should be a major, can't be ignored, wakeup call for the church of today to get back to the biblical basics. The 30 plus congregations mentioned in the New Testament ceased to exist; some even after being warned and confronted by the Lord Himself (Cf. 7 churches of Asia, Revelation 1-3).

All hands need to be on the deck of the "Old Ship of Zion" as we man-the-sails to correct our present location and get back to the course outlined for us in the Scriptures. "Hear this, now hear this, we're on our Master's course headed toward Home."

FOR THOUGHT AND DISCUSSION

1. Why is the first place to start getting back to basics is with exploring the fundamentals—first principles—of the Scriptures?

2. What are some obvious signs that we have drifted from the anchor of Scripture? As congregations? As individual Christians?

3. How can we get back to exploring the Scriptures? When can we?

4. How will you get back to exploring the first principles of Scriptures?

5. Why is authority the key issue in exploring and applying verses?

6. Discuss Hebrews 5:8, 9.

7. What additional observations do you have?

8. ARE YOU READY TO GET BACK TO THE BASICS IN SCRIPTURE?

Part 3

THE CORE E's OF OUR MISSION

E-1

ENTHRONING GOD

The first line in the Holy Bible is, *"In the beginning God" (Genesis 1:1).* The starting place for a serious and more in-depth study of back to the basic is GOD. Stop and think for a minute the state we would be in if we leave God out of our lives:

(1) Leave God out and you have no "Alpha-Omega" (Revelation 1:11).

(2) Leave God out and we have no eternal plan of salvation (Ephesians 1:3-7).

(3) Leave God out and there is no eternal love for sinners (John 3:16; Romans 5:1-7).

(4) Leave God out and there is no amazing grace that provides salvation for the lost sinner (Ephesians 2:1-8).

(5) Leave God out and we can't sing "How Great Thou Art".

(6) Leave God out and Jesus is not "Immanuel"—*"God with us" (Matthew 1:23).*

(7) Leave God out and the grave is the end of us all (1 Corinthians 15:50-55).

(8) Leave God out and we have no eternal basics to go back to truths revealed in inspired Scripture (2 Timothy 3:15-17).

(9) Leave God out and there is no hope (Romans 8:24).

(10)Leave God out and there is no crown of life (Revelation 2:10).

What are some additional blessings we wouldn't have if we leave God out?____

____

____

GOD ALWAYS MAKES THE DIFFERENCE

In my opinion a great place to see the difference God makes, regardless of the situation, is in the Book of Isaiah. The first 39 chapters are filled with the judgment upon the moral and idolatrous people in Judah and Jerusalem. Take a pause and read chapters 1 through 5.

If we are shocked and repulsed by the sins described in the texts, can we imagine how Isaiah must have felt to not only witness it firsthand but be called to go and preach against the sins of God's rebellious people? Think about this for a moment. But wait—there is HOPE—God shows up on His throne and Isaiah sees Him in a glorious vision:

"In the year that King Uzziah died, I SAW the Lord sitting on His throne, high and lifted up, and the train of His robe filled the temple. Above it stood seraphim; each one had six wings: with two he covered his face, with two he covered his feet, and with two he flew. And one cried to another and said: 'Holy, holy is the Lord of hosts; the whole earth is full of His glory!' And the posts of the door were shaken by the

VOICE of him who cried out, and the house what filled with smoke. So I said: 'Woe is me, for I am undone! Because I am a man of unclean lips, and I dwell in the midst of people of unclean lips; for MY EYES have SEEN THE KING, the Lord of hosts.' Then one of the seraphim flew to me, having in his hand a live coal which he had taken with the tongs from the altar. And he touched my mouth with it, and said: 'Behold, this has touched your lips; your iniquity is taken away, and your sins purged'" (Isaiah 6:1-7).

Wow! Amazing! What a vision and forgiveness extended to the prophet by God. It all started when Isaiah SAW God high and holy on His throne. But the story has only just begun. Now that he has a fresh vision of God and forgiveness of his sins, the prophet is ready to accept a mission call from God. All missions start with God.

Here is how Isaiah described the call: *"Also I heard a voice of the Lord, saying; 'Whom shall I SEND, and who will GO FOR US?' Then I said, 'Here AM I! SEND ME.' Then He said, 'Go and tell this people'"*. *(Isaiah 6:8, 9)*. No questions, arguments, etc. Isaiah was on his way.

OBSERVATION: We will not even start with the basics much less get back to them if we don't ENTHRONE God in our mind, heart, soul, and strength (Cf. Mark 12:28-35). I know Christians will, at least most will, agree with this observation. However, an agreement is one thing and actual practice is another (Cf. James 1:21-27). It is obvious that we must first ENTHRONE God if we desire to go BACK TO BASICS.

THE DANGER OF TRYING TO MANAGE GOD

From Adam and Eve in the Garden until today and tomorrow, if we are given a tomorrow, humans have been trying to manage God. They have not only tried to create Him in their own image but even lower than their image. Paul addressed this in Romans 1:22-24:

"Professing to be wise, they became fools, and CHANGED the glory of the INCORRUPTIBLE God into an image made like corruptible man— and birds and four-footed animals and creeping things. THEREFORE God gave them up to uncleanness, in the lusts of their hearts, to dishonor their bodies among themselves" (Cf. Psalm 115:1-8).

In his dynamic and eye-opening book, *The Trivialization of God*, Donald W. McCullough writes: *"Visit a church on Sunday morning— almost any church will do—and you will likely find a congregation comfortably relating to a deity who fits nicely within precise doctrinal positions, or who lend almighty support to social crusades, or who conforms to individual spiritual experiences. But you will not find much awe or sense of mystery. The only sweaty palms will be those of the preacher unsure whether the sermon will go over ... The New Testament warns us, 'offer to God acceptable worship with reverence and awe; for indeed our God is a consuming fire' (Hebrews 12:28, 29)." (Page 13, NavPress, 1995, Colorado Springs, CO 80935).*

God must be enthroned in His rightful place of honor, glory, and authority over US. We are his workmanship; He is not ours.

TRYING TO OUTGUESS OR UNDERMINE GOD

Then there is Jonah! Man does his name ring a bell. He was the prophet who thought he knew better than God when it came to going on a preaching mission. First, he must have reasoned that God shouldn't be showing mercy to the wicked Ninevites. Second, he was only one man, a lone voice crying out against a city of thousands; the odds of success were less than zero. Therefore when God called and gave Jonah his assignment, like many today who think they know what is best or more than God, Jonah buys a ticket on a ship bound for Tarshish; a place where he could get away from God and void his mission.

I'm sure you know the story, most kids in Bible classes know it. God didn't rescind His command. After a dunking in the sea, a few days in the stomach of a great fish, stinking, hungry, and wet, God gives the reluctant prophet who thought he knew what was best, a second chance. Jonah obeyed but still grumbled and complained (Cf. Jonah 4:1-11). The prophet cared more for plants than he did people.

Back to basics demands that we ENTHRONE God in our every thought, emotion, and behavior. Remember, Jesus said, *"And this is ETERNAL LIFE, that they KNOW YOU, the only true God, AND Jesus Christ whom YOU sent" (John 17:3).* It is personal knowledge of God.

We are commanded by God in His word to go to "wicked Nineveh" that lies in darkness (1 John 5:19). A world being led by Satan who is *"seeking whom he may devour" (1 Peter 5:8).*

THE HEART IS WHERE GOD MUST BE ENTHRONED

In his message on Mars Hill to the philosophers, Paul said this about how important our concept of God is: *"God, who made the world and everything in it, since He is the Lord of HEAVEN AND EARTH, does not dwell in temples made with hands. Nor is He worshipped with men's hands, as though He needed anything, since HE GIVES to ALL LIFE, breath, and all things"* (Acts 17:24, 25).

Since God cannot be enthroned in anything made by the hands of men, where is He to be enthroned? The answer is in the HEART of each person. Jesus affirmed this when He answered the scribe's question about which is the greatest commandment of all? (Mark 12:28).

*"Jesus answered him, 'The FIRST of ALL the commandments is: "Hear, O Israel, the Lord our God, the Lord is one. And you SHALL love the Lord your God with ALL your **heart**, with all your **soul**, with all your **mind**, and with all your **strength**. This is the FIRST commandment. And the second, like it, is this: You shall LOVE your neighbor as yourself. There is no other commandment GREATER THAN THESE'"* (Mark 12:29-31). How simple! But oh how challenging and demanding.

Notice the 7 points in Mark 12:29-31:

(1) The Lord is ONE—there are no other Gods—1 is less than 2.

(2) We are to LOVE Him—because He first loved us.

(3) We are to love Him with all our HEART—not 99%.

(4) We are to love Him with all our SOUL—our internal and external being. Not some, part, a little but ALL.

(5) We are to love Him with all our MIND—which is set on Him (Colossians 3:2)

(6) We are to love God with all our STRENGTH. No strength left for self, others, or things—we borrow from His strength.

(7) And we are to love our NEIGHBOR as ourselves. This is the final proof of obedience to this commandment.

From this brief lesson, it should be clear that it's not biblically possible to return to the basics without starting by ENTHRONING God. Remember, *"IN THE BEGINNING GOD."*

FOR THOUGHT AND DISCUSSION

1. How Galatians 6 does: 7 relate to this study? Discuss.

2. How does Malachi 3:8 relate to this study? Discuss.

3. How does Psalm 14:1 relate to this study? Discuss.

4. How is God trivialized today in and out of the church?

5. What are some modern forms of idolatry which hinder us from worshipping God in spirit and in truth?

6. What additional observations do you have?

7. How will you intentionally enthrone God in your life 24-7-365?

EXALTING CHRIST

In a survey of Christians, a large number were asked WHY they attended church services. The answers were interesting. Some were:

1. *It is my duty as a Christian to attend church.*
2. *It is a habit I've had since I was a child.*
3. *I enjoy the fellowship, singing and seeing my friends.*
4. *I attend to be an example to my kids and others.*
5. *To break the weekly cycle of loneliness.*
6. *To partake of the Lord's Supper which is commanded.*
7. *I am commanded to attend and not to do so is sinful.*
8. *I am afraid of going to hell or missing heaven.*
9. *Honestly, I'm not sure...I just do.*
10. *Honestly, to obey the command in Hebrews 10:25.*

What is your answer to this question: Why do you attend church?

____

____

Looking over the above answers what would you say is missing? No one said their reason for attending was JESUS. Granted some may have had that as the subconscious catalysis for their answers, and perhaps some didn't. Either way, Christ was not mentioned as the reason.

Don't you find, as I do, it very interesting that no one said his or her **love** for Christ was the reason for attending the assemblies of the *ekklesia (community)?*

By now, hopefully, you are understanding the reason why exalting Christ is the second **E** in our study of back to basics. Christ is the *"alpha and omega"—the beginning and the end* of the gifts, blessings, and promises of God to His church family. *"They shall call His name JESUS, for it is He who shall save His people"* (Matthew 1:21).

REASONS FOR EXALTING CHRIST

There's a verse in a once-popular hymn written in the 1800s by Johnson Oatman, which says,

> *"Don't exalt the preacher, don't exalt the pew,*
>
> *Preach the Gospel simple, full and free;*
>
> *Prove him and you will find that promise*
>
> *I'll draw all men unto Me."*

FIRST, we exalt Christ by LIFTING him up. The Scripture this hymn is based on is Jesus' words in John 12:32: *"And I, if I am LIFTED UP from the earth, will DRAW all PEOPLES to Myself."* In verse 33 we are told what Jesus was making reference to in this verse: *"This He said, signifying by what DEATH He would die."* Jesus promised that His death on the cross would be the sufficient power to DRAW all people to him (Cf. Matthew 28:18-20; Romans 1:14-16; 2 Thessalonians 2:14, etc.).

SECOND, Christ's name is above every name both in heaven and on earth. "Therefore God also has highly EXALTED Him and given Him the name which is ABOVE every name, that at the name of Jesus EVERY knee should bow, of those in heaven, and of those on earth, and of those under the earth, and that EVERY tongue should CONFESS that Jesus Christ is Lord, to the glory of God the Father' (Philippians 2:9-11). We honor His name by not taking it in vain, blaspheming it, or using it as a swear word.

THIRD, we exalt Christ by accepting and obeying His authority. He has been given all authority in heaven and on earth (Matthew 28:18-20). "[T]hough He was a Son, yet He LEARNED obedience by the things which he suffered. And having been made PERFECT, He became the AUTHOR of eternal salvation to ALL who OBEY Him" (Hebrews 5:8, 9). We exalt Christ by accepting His authorship of our salvation when we obey Him.

FOURTH, we exalt Christ when we pray by recognizing and utilizing Him as the one MEDIATOR between us and our heavenly Father. *"For there is one God and one MEDIATOR between God and man, the Man Christ Jesus, who gave Himself a ransom for all, to be testified in due time"* (1 Timothy 2:5, 6). It is by the authority—"In Christ's name"—as He serves as our Mediator that we exalt Christ when we pray.

FIFTH, we exalt Christ by acknowledging that He is King of kings: "[T]*hat you keep His commandment without spot, blameless until our Lord Jesus Christ's appearing, which he will manifest in His own time, He who is BLESSED and only Potentate, the KING of kings and Lord of lords" (1 Timothy 6:14, 15; Cf. Revelation 1:5; 17:14).* What a blessing to have Christ as our King and be able to honor Him 24-7-365.

SIXTH, we exalt Christ by obeying what our heavenly Father commanded on the Mount of Transfiguration: *"While he (Peter) was still speaking, behold a bright cloud overshadowed them; and suddenly a voice came from out of the cloud, saying, 'This is My beloved Son, in whom I am well pleased. Hear HIM!'" (Matthew 17:1-5).* There are hundreds of voices chattering in the world and seeking our attention, but we must listen to only one—the VOICE of Jesus.

SEVENTH, we exalt Christ by accepting, believing, and walking in assurance because He understands our trials and struggles. *"For we do not have a High Priest who cannot sympathize with our weaknesses, but was in ALL POINTS tempted as we are, yet without sin. Let us, therefore, come BOLDLY to the throne of grace, that we may obtain mercy and find grace to help in TIME OF NEED" (Hebrews 4:15, 16).* As the hymn says, *"Jesus knows all about my troubles."*

EIGHTH, we exalt Christ because He is IMMANUEL—God with us: *"Behold, the virgin shall be with child, and bear a Son, and they shall call His name Immanuel, which is translated 'GOD WITH US'" (Matthew 1:23).* This is what Thomas confessed: *"And Thomas answered and said to Him, 'My Lord and my God!'" (John 20:28).* Jesus is not one of the boys or just another teacher, He is GOD. Read Colossians 1:15.

NINTH, we exalt Christ as the architect, builder, and Savior of the church (*ekklesia*), which is His body (Read Matthew 16:13-20). *"And*

He is before all things, and in Him, all things consist. And he is the HEAD of the body, the church, who is the beginning, the firstborn from the dead, that in all things He may have the preeminence" (Colossians 1:17, 18).

TENTH, we exalt Christ by loving Him and KEEPING His commandments: *"If you love Me, keep my commandments"* (John 14:15). *"You are My friends if YOU DO whatever I command you"* (John 15:14). It is out of LOVE, not fear, that we keep the commandments of Christ. They are not burdensome.

FOR THOUGHT AND DISCUSSION

1. What does the word EXALT mean? How does it apply to Christ?
2. Why is the exaltation of Christ second as a basic doctrine?
3. Which of the above 10 reasons/ways to exalt Christ is the most overlooked or neglected? Why?
4. How does the Gospel relate to Jesus' promise to draw all men to Himself? Discuss.
5. What role does loving Christ play in exalting Christ?
6. What are some additional ways a Christian can exalt Christ?

    (a)____

    (b)____

    (c)____

7. What additional observations do you have?
8. How will you intentionally exalt Christ today? Tomorrow?

EDIFYING THE BODY OF CHRIST

Charlie's name had appeared on the church's absentee list for several weeks, which wasn't like him. He was always faithful in attendance, especially on Sunday morning. When a member of the visitation team visited Charlie at home, he asked him several questions. One was, "Why haven't you been attending church recently? What's wrong? Is there anything we can help you with?"

After several minutes sharing answers which were obviously evasive, the visiting brother said, "Now come on Charlie; something is wrong. Share it and we can pray about it and find an answer in God's word. I want to help, we are brothers in Christ."

After a few moments of silence, Charlie said, "Okay, I'll tell you. I quit attending because every time I left the church I felt discouraged. All I was hearing was how bad I was, how terrible other churches were, and I needed to give more. I know, I must have a bad or sinful attitude. But don't you think there should be some encouragement along with the discouragement; a little balance would be great."

We can analyze Charlie's remarks and poke holes in them with such remarks as, "Well, if Charlie loved the Lord he wouldn't let those things bother him; he must have needed to hear those lessons, why else would he feel guilty?" "You know the Bible says "reprove, rebuke, and exhort", Charlie needed to open his heart and receive the truth.

I don't want to get bogged down in debating the right or wrong, etc. of Charlie's issues. I know one thing for sure, whether right or wrong, God knows his heart, there are hundreds, maybe thousands, who are in the same mode as Charlie—they have stopped attending church. Why? (Cf. Hebrews 4:12)

Listening to members, visiting those who are delinquent, and re-searching surveys, I have compiled the following reasons why Christians tend to stay away from church because of DISCOURAGEMENT:

1. *I can't live up to the standards.*
2. *The church expects too much from me.*
3. *I don't seem to be able to do anything right.*
4. *I'm not smart enough to understand all those big words.*
5. *I've been bad too long…I don't seem to make any progress.*
6. *The preacher is always beating up on other churches.*
7. *I've been accused of not loving the Lord or being converted.*
8. *They're always dealing with messiness…never joy or grace.*
9. *Leaders are blind and keep us in ditches.*
10. *The atmosphere is like a morgue or mortuary.*

I'm sure you and I both could provide deep biblical and spiritual answers or replies to each of these "reasons" or complaints. But the truth is for the persons making them they are "real reasons" being used by Satan to discourage them to the point of drifting away and finally back into Satan's camp (Cf. 2 Peter 2:18-22).

THE MISSION OF EDIFICATION

Regardless of age, education, financial standing, etc. when a person obeys the Gospel he/she is *"born of water and Spirit (Cf. John 3:1-8). Spiritually speaking he/she is a "babe in Christ in need of milk and not strong meat" (2 Peter 2:1-3; Hebrews 5:12-6:8).*

Why do we expect from new babes in Christ what God does not expect? It may be that we don't understand the third basic **E** in our mission: edification. In writing to a church with spiritual babies the apostle Paul outlined the responsibilities of leaders to EDIFY and EQUIP the church for ministry and growth into Christ-likeness (Ephesians 4:10-16). A major goal was for the congregation to *EDIFY ITSELF IN LOVE (4:16).*

What does it mean to *EDIFY?* The basic idea in English is to *"be instructive or informative in ways, both with words and actions that improve the mind or behavior; to uplift; enlightenment, providing moral or intellectual support."* The Greek word which appears in some form in the KJV 20 times is, <u>oikodomeo</u> which means *"to build, to build up".* And was applied to constructing a physical building, used in Scripture to refer to *building up a person—Christian—spiritually. Here are some verses which stress the importance of edification for churches and each Christian:*

1 Timothy 1:3, 4: *"As I urged you when I went into Macedonia, remain in Ephesus that you may charge some that they teach no other doctrine nor give heed to fables and endless genealogies, which cause dispute rather than GODLY EDIFICATION which is in faith."*

Acts 9:31: *"Then the churches throughout all Judea, Galilee, and Samaria had peace and was EDIFIED. And walking in the fear of the Lord and in the comfort of the Holy Spirit, they grew."*

1 Corinthians 14:5: *"I wish you all spoke with tongues, but even more that you prophesied; for he who prophesies is greater than he who speaks with tongues, unless indeed he interprets, that the CHURCH may receive EDIFICATION."*

1 Corinthians 14:12: *"Even so you, since you are zealous for spiritual gifts, let it be for the EDIFICATION of the church that you seek to excel."*

1 Corinthians 14:26: *"How is it then, brethren? Whenever you come together, each of you has a psalm, has a teaching, has a tongue, has a revelation, has an interpretation. Let ALL THINGS be done for EDIFICATION.*

It is clear that the Lord intends for His followers to be EDIFIED—built up in the faith—not in worldliness, philosophy, or speculations, etc. The commanded edification is not determined by a "meet my needs" approach which is so popular today as churches are advertising a promise to "meeting the needs" of attendees. It is God Who determines what our needs are, both in and out of the church. Jeremiah wrote: "O Lord, I know the way of man is not in himself; it is not in man who walks to direct his own steps. O Lord correct me, but with justice..." (Jeremiah 10:23, 24).

NEGLECTING THE PROPER CARE AND FEEDING OF INFANTS

Almost daily if not weekly we hear news reports of a child or children being neglected, abused, and even killed by a parent or parents. Another tragedy that rarely makes the news is the neglect at birth and during the growth period of children.

Can you imagine how ridiculous, sinful, and criminal it would be for a set of parents to have a newborn child and just leave it alone to fan for itself—to feed itself, change its own diapers, learn to walk and talk all by itself? Oh, the parents would occasionally look in on the infant, play tickle and goo-goo with the child. The infant would die because of neglect.

Then there's the set of parents who give only the basic and minimum attention and care for the infant. The child grows slowly and has a number of health issues and struggles to adulthood but with childish skills. In time the child dies because it was neglected in the early growing years when attention was essential.

Our third family smothers their new infant with all kinds of food, responds to every whimper, toys, and gadgets, and as he grows encourages him to gorge on junk food and choose his own entertainment. It's what he wants that matters—his needs must be met.

While these examples may be in what we call "the world" they provide an intro into the need for the care and feeding of spiritual babes in the church today. Persons are baptized and, sadly, are left on their own to grow into the *"fullness of the measure of Christ."* They come to the cafeteria Sunday morning where various spiritual meals are delivered but not fully ingested and digested. Many survive because of the determination of the physical or carnal man to keep the commitment. However, the inner man who must be cared for as a "babe in Christ" is neglected.

DIET, EXERCISE, AND ENVIRONMENT FOR EDIFYING

It is the responsibility of the Shepherds to lead, care for, and feed the sheep in their flock. Baby sheep don't/can't feed baby sheep. It requires a planned strategy for properly edifying each sheep in the flock. The "old rams" have different needs than the "baby lambs." It takes elders who are watchful, educated, and experienced to properly care for and feed the sheep. Here are some supportive Scriptures of these truths:

Acts 20:28: *"Therefore take heed to yourselves and to all the flock among which the Holy Spirit has made you OVERSEERS, to SHEPHERD the church of God which He purchased with His own blood."* Sadly, Paul's words to the Ephesian elders didn't last too long because we read in Revelation 2:1-7 where the church had *"left its first love."*

1 Peter 5:2: *"Shepherd the flock of God which is among you, serving as overseers, not by compulsion but willingly, not for dishonest gain but eagerly."* The elders are responsible for seeing to it that the lambs and older sheep are properly cared for and protected 24-7-365.

In 1 Timothy 3:1-7 and Titus 1:5-9 the apostle Paul gives the various qualifications and works God expects from elders of His flock. Therefore, they are responsible for EDIFYING the sheep—new and older members of the *ekklesia (church).*

When Jesus commanded that followers *"make disciples" (Matthew 28:18-20),* He was requiring that education, training, and leadership be provided for His sheep—young and old. This requires planning and implementing a plan.

THE EDIFYING RESPONSIBILITY OF EVERY MEMBER

While it is true that elders, preachers, and teachers have the primary responsibility for edifying the church, Scriptures make it clear that EVERY member—by reason of time—has a responsibility to encourage and edify **"one another."** In fact, there are over 52 specific "one another" Scriptures in the New Testament illustrating the content and ways to obey the passages. Here are some mutual ways we EDIFY each other in the church:

1. Members should care for one another (1 Corinthians 12:25).

2. Members should bear each other's burdens (Galatians 6:2).

3. Members should teach one another (Colossians 3:16).

4. Members should exhort one another (Hebrews 3:13; 10:24).

5. Members should use hospitality one to another (1 Peter 4:9).

6. Members should forebear one another in love (Ephesians 4:2).

7. Members should forgive one another (Ephesians 4:32).

8. Members comfort one another (1 Thessalonians 4:18).

1. How were you cared for as a "new babe" in Christ?

2. Why is there a tendency to overlook the need for special care and feeding of new converts?

3. How does your congregation tend, guard, and feed a new Christian?

4. What is the difference between feeding a new babe in Christ milk and strong meat?

5. What are some ways to create a new converts class and feeding periods to help new Christians grow?

6. Do most members understand and participate in their role and responsibility for edifying other members of the body?

7. What additional thoughts do you have?

8. How will you intentionally become more involved in edifying yourself and others?

E-4

EQUIPPING THE SAINTS

A group of senior managers, supervisors, Vice Presidents, and the CFO were having their biannual meeting in which they were discussing what the company needed. Some suggested new screening procedures for future employees, some suggested pay raises, a few advocated for more vacation time, some wanted a better health plan, etc. When asked was there any more suggestions, the janitorial supervisor dressed in his blue work clothes replied, "Yes, I think what we need around here is for somebody to go to work!" I've often wondered how that suggestion was received. How about in a congregation today?

In our traditional and eternal business meetings, we are famous for discussing what the congregation needs: programs, volunteers, doctrinal issues, better lighting and sound, updated bulletin and membership directory, budget issues, etc. When what most congregations need is for "somebody to go to work." Don't you agree?

Check this out. In most congregations, 20% of the members do all the work and the 80% receive the benefits, even wanting to dictate how and what the 20% are, or are not, doing. It's the old Pareto Law.

As we have continually touched on in our previous studies the church has a dynamic mission which must be pursued by each member—not the 20%... based on *"by reason of time you ought to be* *teachers" (Hebrews 5:12-6:3).*This is contrary to some zealous proponents of "As soon as you pop up out of the baptismal waters you ought to pop over to your best friend and share the Good News". I'm not saying this is wrong; only that it's challenging for a "baby Christian" to be involved in "birthing a baby Christian."

Jesus spent approximately 3 ½ years selecting, training, mentoring, and educating His Apostles to lead the *ekklesia* in her mission after He returned to heaven.

What comes to mind when you hear the word **EQUIP?** The English word is defined as follows: *Equip (verb): to supply with necessary items for a particular purpose: a person, place, or thing; to prepare someone mentally, physically, or spiritually for a specific task or situation; to give adequate provisions; e.g. boot camp is designed to help equip recruits to become effective soldiers," etc.*

Based on the definition of EQUIP it is obvious that there is a need for EQUIPPERS. You can't EQUIP another person in all the required disciplines without being an equipper who by reason of time, training, and experience has become equipped. Oh, you may teach some theories gained from a textbook or from a quick indoctrination class. I have seen novices try to equip others when they needed to be equipped themselves; especially among preachers, etc. The key to working as an effective equipper is *"by reason of time"* the knowledge, understanding, skills, and experiences have been developed.

SOME DISCIPLINES RELATED TO EQUIPPING

God has placed *"each member in the body just where He wants that member" (1 Corinthians 12:18).* He has designated certain works for men and certain works for women. Each member functions according to the development of their gifts, training, and placement in the body. According to 1 Corinthians 12:12-31 each member has being assigned a core function; equipping will help each member discover and develop the core gift as well as other sub-gifts that will need to be developed. Again, it takes TIME and commitment by both the equipper and the member being equipped.

Here is an overview of some of the key areas where equipping for ministry needs to focus:

1. Christians must be equipped, through self-motivation, to keep in mind the self-denial commitment they made to follow Christ (Matthew 16:24). It is not optional.

2. Christians need to be equipped with planned procedures to think and act biblically in daily life (Proverbs 23:7; Philippians 2:5-8). To also have the right thinking agenda (Philippians 4:7-9).

3. Christians need to be equipped to continually keep in memory the Gospel (Read 1 Corinthians 15:1-11 for the facts). This requires developing memorization skills.

4. Christians need to be equipped with the skills to know how to study the Bible on their own (2 Timothy 2:15, KJV).

5. Christians need to be equipped with knowledge relative to how to worship God in spirit and in truth (John 4:23, 24).

6. Christians need to be equipped with knowledge and skills relative to being good stewards (1 Corinthians 4:1-3).

7. Christians must be equipped relative to how to *"behave in the house (church) of God"* (1 Timothy 3:15).

8. Christians must be biblically equipped with ways, means, and knowledge on how to teach the lost (Mark 16:15, 16; 2 Timothy 2:1-3).

9. Christians must be properly equipped to *"fight the good fight of faith"* (Ephesians 6:10-20).

10. Christians must be spiritually and biblically equipped to *"defend the faith"* (Jude 3; 1 Peter 3:15).

11. Christians must be equipped with knowledge and skills on how to encourage others (Hebrews 10:24).

12. Christians need to study and be equipped with the skills to be a "prayer warriors" in the Lord's Army (Luke 11:1-4).

13. Christians need to be equipped with how to have the assurance of their salvation (1 John 1:7-9; 5:13).

14. Christians need to be equipped with what the Bible says about how to handle differences with others (Matthew 18:15-20).

15. Christians need to be equipped with knowledge and skills relative to how to be leaders in the church, on the job, and in the

home—how to be servants (Ephesians 5:22; 6:4; 1 Timothy 4:12, etc.)

16. Christians need to be equipped relative to how to lead a balanced and stress-free life (Mark 6:30-32).

17. Christians need to be equipped with ways and means to communicate in love (Ephesians 4:15; 1 Corinthians 13:12, 13).

These 17 identifications are only a few of the qualities every Christian should be equipped, by reason of time, to have in his or her life. They are all related to the spiritual growth process. None of these virtues will happen by chance over a period of time or by luck. They must be identified, desired, and committed to before they become realities.

As a Christian works to equip himself with these qualities there will be times of discouragements, setbacks, and disappointments. Memorize these words by Paul, *"Let us not grow weary in well-doing"* (Galatians 6:9). Practice *"renewing your mind every day"* (Colossians 3:2; Romans 12:1, 2).

SUGGESTIONS FOR EQUIPPING

Here are a few suggestions for developing an equipping program:

1. Study the major skills a Christian must be equipped to perform.

2. Develop qualified teachers who will be equippers.

3. Communicate to the new as well as the older converts the need for being equipped—"New converts class."

4. Since there are numerous areas equipping is related to, it will take time and work—develop a schedule—be creative.

5.   A rotating mentoring program may be developed.

FOR THOUGHT AND DISCUSSION

1.   How effective has your congregation been in equipping the membership for ministry? What is your proof?

2.   Why have some congregations neglected to equip the membership for ministry?

3.   What percentage of your congregation does the work? Why?

4.   How do we confuse physical and age maturity with spiritual maturity? How does this relate to equipping?

5.   How thoroughly do you feel your equipping has been since you became a Christian? Are there any weak spots? Why?

6.   What is the content of your "new converts" class? How was it developed?

7.   What would be some benefits for every member of the church to go through the basics of equipping mentioned in this lesson? Why?

8.   What are some possible dangers of novices trying to equip babes in Christ?

9.   What additional observations do you have?

10. How will you intentionally use this lesson in your life and ministry?

EVANGELISTIC MISSION

Wake five Christians from sleep and ask them, *"Quick! What is the mission of the local church?"* I'm not a betting man but I venture to say the answer would be either *soul-winning, evangelism, sharing the Gospel, converting the lost,* or some other words related to obeying the Great Commission.

Have you ever wondered why there is no account of a "soul-winning" or "evangelism training class" mentioned in the book of Acts or the Epistles? Why no one is rebuked, shamed, or fired because he wasn't evangelistic enough? Yet, there is evidence that those who were scattered abroad went everywhere preaching the word (Acts 8:1-8). I guess when the word is shut up in your heart like a fire, like Jeremiah had (Jeremiah 20:9), you don't have to be coaxed, prodded, shamed, or commanded to share the Good News; snatching them out of the fire is a natural response of love and caring (Jude 20-23).

The apostle Paul who was the most evangelistic preacher, as far as we know, in the early church, wasn't committed to saving souls just because he was commanded to do so. No! He had a heart-felt burden and desire for the salvation of his countrymen. *"Brethren, my HEART'S DESIRE and prayer to God for Israel is they may be saved" (Rom.10:1).*

Through the years we have done a fairly decent job in planting the seed of evangelistic awareness in the thinking of most church members, but in most cases that awareness hasn't led to hardly any results in the lives of many members.

The roar is loud in the stands but no one will get on the field where the hard knocks and rejection occur. And the saddest point of all is that none evangelistic leaders will fire a preacher for not being evangelistic enough. This and other reasons are why we must return to the BASICS related to the "first principles" of sharing the Gospel with the lost, biblically referred to as evangelism and preaching the word.

SOME MISUNDERSTANDINGS ABOUT EVANGELISM

In my 52-plus years of fulltime ministry, I have seen the emphasis given to evangelism rise and fall in congregations. In the 60s and 70s, there were evangelism workshops, seminars, and conferences occurring every week somewhere in the brotherhood. Our colleges had frequent lectureships on evangelism. Across the nation we had large coliseums rented for soul-winning campaigns; national TV and radio programs. Brotherhood papers printed the number of conversions from Gospel meetings, etc. We were considered one of the fastest-growing churches in America. Sadly, this is no longer the case.

From all the evangelistic activity back then an interesting phenomenon has occurred, either consciously or unconsciously, which has produced some of the following misunderstandings of evangelism, especially when compared with the Scriptures. Here are, in my opinion, a few of these misunderstandings:

1. The sole purpose of the church's existence is to save souls. As we are seeing in this study evangelism is not the ONLY reason—the major reason is to *GLORIFY GOD (Ephesians 3:21)*.

2. While each soul saved represents a number, evangelism is not a numbers game or a crusade for numbers. In some areas, congregations are in competition to see who can "win the most souls." Numbers matter!

3. Evangelism is not an occasional effort determined by a date on the congregation's yearly calendar and promoted as "Our annual meeting."

4. Evangelism is not the work of an expert or a few experts which may occur through importing for a week or two "campaign workers" who leave once the week is over.

5. Evangelism is not the sole work of a hired preacher who goes out into the "highways and byways and compels the lost to come in."

6. Evangelism is not a building centered effort; for persons desiring salvation, he/she will be invited to come to the building.

7. Evangelism is a complex communication activity that one must be highly trained to participate in. You must know how to debate, answer every question, and never say "I don't know."

8. Evangelism is not a marketing tool to advertise the church and entice people who are lost, and saved, to attend.

9. Evangelism's central purpose is not to promote messages that meet the "psychological needs or marital needs" of the members or community. The purpose of evangelism is to present the Gospel: the life, death, burial, and resurrection of Christ as the solution to man's sin problem (1 Corinthians 15:3, 4).

10. Evangelism is not just a topic of study from time to time; a time when a brief period of excitement occurs and then wanes until the next pep rally.

11. It is not a book produced by man in which he tries to bypass the purity of the Gospel message preached by Peter on the Day of Pentecost; by telling "his and other people's stories."

I'm sure some readers will disagree with some of these observations, which is okay. However, one thing, hopefully, we agree on and that is we need to restore the biblical emphasis we see in the early church on sharing the GOSPEL.

MOTIVATION FOR EVANGELISM

Now that we have taken a brief look at some possible misunderstandings about evangelism, let's turn our attention to what should motivate the church to place a high and continual emphasis on preaching the Gospel. Keep in mind that motivation is something that is produced by each person within his/her own soul, and external stimuli may ignite the inner flame. Here are some motivations for evangelism:

1. **The value of the soul** should be an incentive for evangelism. *"For what will it profit a man if he gains the whole world, and lose his OWN SOUL? Or what shall a man give in EXCHANGE for his SOUL? (Mark 8:36, 37).*

2. **The fate of a lost soul** is a dynamic incentive for evangelism. In Luke 16:23, 24, we read the fate of a rich man who died lost: *"And being in torments in Hades, he lifted up his eyes and saw Abraham afar off, and Lazarus in his bosom. Then he cried and said, 'Father Abraham, have mercy on me… for I am tormented in these flames.'"*

3. **Thankfulness for one's own salvation** is a major incentive to share the Gospel with the lost. As a hungry man who found the Bread of Life, Jesus Christ, you want to tell others where they too may find the free BREAD—the gift of eternal life. (Matthew 4:1-6; John 6:48).

4. **The cost and sacrifice for salvation** is a marvelous incentive for planting the Gospel seed of salvation in the heart of a person (Luke 8:11-15; Matthew 26:28; 1 Peter 1:18, 19).

5. **The love we have for Christ** is a major motivation for obeying the Great Commission to evangelize, which He gave to His followers (John 14:15; Matthew 28:18-20). We don't love sin but we love the sinner—Jesus died to save sinners (Luke 19:10).

6. **Helping Christ expand and fill His community** is a great biblical incentive to share the Gospel with the lost. Go back for refresher thoughts on what we learned about the *ekklesia* and how it relates to glorifying God (John 14:6; Matthew 21:13; Hebrews 3:4-6).

7. **The growth of the spiritual family** is made possible by evangelism which creates new joint-heirs and adopted family members who care for one another. This should be an incentive for evangelism.

These are only 7 motivations for evangelism; there are many more. Can you think of 3 more?

1).____

2).____

3).____

As the saved, we should be highly motivated to evangelize.

METHODS OF EVANGELISM

Biblically speaking evangelism consists of the following factors as taught by Jesus in the Parable of the Sower (Luke 8:5-10; 11-15).

1. A lost person. His/her heart is the soil into which the Gospel seed must be planted. A lost person is separated from God (Isaiah 59:1, 2). Sin originates in the heart (James 1:13-16).

2. Evangelism occurs when a Christian (a sower) sows the seed in the heart of another person (a sinner). Angels don't do it. Let's take a closer look at Luke 8:5-15 (Please read it).

3. A sower (a Christian) sows the seed in the soil—heart (8:5).

4. A heart receives it but Satan steals the seed (word) (8:12).

5. Seed lodges in a heart that is faithful for a little while (8:13).

6. Another heart destroys the seed because of worries (8:14).

7. The 4th heart is patient and brings forth fruit—saved (8:15).

The apostle Paul outlines in 1 Corinthians 3:6, 7, the conversion process as it relates to sowing the seed:

✓ I PLANTED (3:6)

✓ Apollos WATERED (3:6)

✓ But God gave the INCREASE (3:6)

God's method doesn't involve gimmicks, human marketing schemes, scare tactics, drama and stories, long and drawn-out presentations. A reading of Peter's Gospel sermon—the very first—on the Day of Pentecost contained approximately 350 words which "pricked hearts" and led to 3000 sinners being baptized into Christ (Acts 2:38; Galatians 3:27). And the establishment of the church (Acts 2:47)

In order to evangelize in harmony with what we see in the New Testament, we must share the Gospel we already know—we've obeyed it, kept it in memory and can/will share it with the lost. This is the simple way of going BACK TO BASICS. No matter how creative a person may become in developing methods and schemes to convert people, God's way of evangelism—one saved sinner telling one lost sinner—where to find the Pearl of Great Princes and the Bread of Life—it's in the Gospel message. (Romans 1:14-16; Romans 10:17).

FOR THOUGHT AND DISCUSSION

1. How do you define evangelism? Share your answer.

2. Why has evangelism been neglected in some churches?

3. Why is the Gospel the message which must be proclaimed to call a person to salvation (Cf. 2 Thessalonians 2:14)?

4. What tends to sidetrack us from practicing evangelism as we see in the early church?

5. Based on Luke 8:5-15, what are some methods we can use to sow the seed? How about watering the seed (1 Corinthians 3:4-6)?

6. Why is evangelism the last thing some congregations do and the first thing they give up?

7. In your opinion how can a congregation return to making evangelism a priority?

8. What role does leadership play in evangelism?

9. What additional thought do you have about this subject?

10. How will you intentionally apply this lesson to your life and ministry?

EXPLOSIVE CHURCH GROWTH & CONVERSIONS

A few weeks ago we had a weekend where the President and staff of World Bible Institute, a mission and educational program sponsored by our congregation, presented an update on how God is blessing this work in various parts of the world. When he reported that in one evangelistic campaign in Africa where 400-plus were baptized in one day, "Amen!" came from those who never say Amen.

It is rare in a statewide campaign for there to be 4, 14, or dare I say 40 during a week or two-week effort to baptize the lost into Christ.

In the first years of my preaching ministry, some of the brotherhood papers would have a section where baptisms were reported. There was a running list of congregations that baptized 100 or more during a year. One year during my 10-year tenure with the White's Ferry Road School of Biblical Studies, the church and school efforts baptized 165. Later in my first two years, 1980, 81, as the preacher for the Newland Street church of Christ, Garden Grove, California, we had 101 baptisms in 12 months. In fact I have a special issue of *Personal Evangelism* magazine (July, Aug., Sept. 1981) which features Newland Street. We were referred to as one of the fastest growing congregations in California.

Obviously things have changed over the years since the 70s, 80s, and 90s. The number of conversions from evangelistic efforts grow smaller each year. Sadly, some congregations have gone for more than a year without a baptism. We can't change yesterday and tomorrow is not promised; today is the only day we have to activate our desires and actions to go back to the basics. The basics we see demonstrated in the first-century church.

THE EXPLOSIVE GROWTH OF THE FIRST CENTURY CHURCH

This **E** is really the second part of the last **E** relating to evangelism. In this lesson, we will see that "Jesus said GO share the Gospel with every creature"—and they could say, "We have done it." This is documented in the Book of Acts and Epistles.

The Book of Acts is not called the Book of Acts because it contained the resolution of the Apostles or first-century church members; it documents their ACTIONS in fulfilling the Great Commission. Here is a quick overview, starting on the Day of Pentecost as the Gospel was being spread in the first-century world by our brethren, the first members of the *ekklesia*.

1. **Started with 3000 on the first day:** *"Then those who gladly received his word were baptized, and that DAY about three thousand were added to them"* (Acts 2:41).

2. **Conversions were occurring daily:** *"[P]raising God and having favor with all the people. And the Lord added to the church*

DAILY those who were being saved" (Acts 2:47).

3. **Multitudes were added to the church:** *"And believers were IN-CREASINGLY ADDED to the Lord, multitudes of both men and women" (Acts 5:14).*

4. **A great many people were added to the church:** *"For he was a good man, full of the Holy Spirit and of faith. And a GREAT many were ADDED to the Lord" (Acts 11:24).*

5. **The preaching of the word increased:** *"But the word of God GREW and multiplied" (Acts 12:24).*

6. **The world couldn't deny the impact of the Gospel:** *"But when they did not find them, they dragged Jason and some brethren to the rulers of the city crying out, 'These who have turned the world upside down have come here too'" (Acts 17:6).*

7. **Converts were showing the fruits of changed lives:** *"And many who had believed came CONFESSING and TELLING their deeds" (Acts 19:18).*

8. **The word was being spread among all the Jews:** *"For we have found this man a plague, a creator of dissension among ALL the JEWS throughout the WORLD, and ringleader of the sect of the Nazarenes" (Acts 24:5).*

9. **The Gospel was shared with leaders:** *"King Agrippa, do you believe the prophets? I know that you DO BELIEVE. Then Agrippa said to Paul, 'You almost persuade me to become a Christian'" (Acts 26:27, 28).*

10. **The Book of Acts closes with the account of Paul's imprison-
ment in Rome and his continuing to preach the Gospel:** *"Then
Paul dwelt two whole years in his own rented house, and received all who came to him, PREACHING the kingdom of God
and TEACHING the things which concern the Lord Jesus Christ
with all CONFIDENCE, no one forbidding him"* (Acts 28:30, 31).

As Christians were scattered the Gospel spread throughout the world as preaching and teaching occurred. In time it was recorded that it had been spread to the whole world:

1. **Colossians 1:23:** *'[I]f indeed you continue in the FAITH,
grounded and steadfast, and are not moved away from the
HOPE of the gospel which you have HEARD, which WAS
PREACHED TO EVERY CREATURE UNDER HEAVEN, of which I,
Paul, became a minister."*

2. **Romans 10:17, 18:** *"So then faith comes by HEARING, and
hearing by the word of God. But I say, have they not HEARD?
Yes indeed: 'Their sound has gone out to ALL THE EARTH, and
their words to the ENDS of the WORLD.'"*

3. **Revelation 7:9:** *"After these things I looked, and behold, a
great multitude which no one could number, of ALL NATIONS,
TRIBES, PEOPLES, and TONGUES, standing before the throne
and before the Lamb, clothed with white robes, with palm
branches in their hands"* (Cf. Isaiah 2:2-4; Matthew 8:11).

Amazing! In approximately 60-plus years the brethren in the first century obeyed Jesus' command. They preached the Gospel to the world. To my knowledge, it hasn't been done since. WHY? It wasn't because they had more going for them than we do.

WHAT THE FIRST CENTURY EKKLESIA (CHURCH) DIDN'T HAVE

Here is an obvious list of things our brethren didn't have in the First Century, that we have, and yet they did what we haven't been able to do—PREACH THE GOSPEL TO THE WORLD.

1. They didn't have a copy of the New Testament. It was being written and circulated on a limited basis among congregations (E.g. Paul's writings). Copies or portions of the Old Testament were in the Temple and some synagogues.

2. They didn't have rapid forms of transportation. Their scattering occurred on foot; a few may have had carts and horses. Jesus was a walker, too.

3. They didn't have special construction projects for collecting money and building "church buildings." The "called out" would meet in homes or other places. The "name of the church" wasn't on any building or billboard.

4. They didn't have any highly educated or recognized scholars occupying pulpits (Which didn't exist). Their leaders were viewed *"As ignorant and unlearned" (Acts 4:11-16).* The Apostles had spent 3-plus years in Jesus' apprentice program.

5. There were no organized praise teams, instruments of music, designated song leaders, or singing 4-part harmony with song-books.

6. They didn't have tax-exemption from the Roman government and a favorable rating from the Better Business Bureau. They had no political connections for special favors.

7. There were no designated clergymen, special bishops, head leaders, managers, staff, bosses; all were servants of one an-other.

8. They conducted no personal work classes, seminars, and work-shops to train members how to be "soul winners." Interest-ingly no one was ever rebuked for not being a "soul winner."

9. There were no "experts" traveling circuits with books, tracts, and visual presentations to help churches reach the lost.

10. They didn't use the postal service to deliver Gospel messages because some were reluctant to deliver in-person to their neighbors and friends.

11. They didn't maintain budgets with a surplus for "emergencies and last-minute projects." (Read 2 Corinthians 8 & 9). There were no savings accounts in the Bank of Rome.

12. There were no denominational alliances or fellowship with pa-gan cults in order to adapt their methods for church growth.

13. There were no structured Bible school programs, youth groups or segregating the members by age, education, etc.

14. There were no Christian colleges, Bible training schools, seminaries, or other higher education programs.

15. Time of services wasn't set in cement for Sunday morning and evening or Wednesday night. Services weren't limited to one hour. The Lord's Supper was the "main event"; not preaching.

16. They didn't have business enterprises operated by congregations in order to raise money and promote programs, etc.

17. They didn't choose an exclusive name to identify themselves from others and post it on a house or other buildings.

18. They didn't accommodate the culture in order to attract visitors and members; they "were in the world but not of the world."

19. They didn't incorporate rituals and music from pagan cults in order to enhance their own emotions and attract outsiders.

20. They never used marketing or business techniques to promote the church and the Gospel. They never had a "consultant" on staff or quarterly evaluator drop in to keep them on track.

NO! I am not saying all of the above things they didn't have should prevent us from prayerfully using some things which may biblically qualify as expediencies. Whatever position you make take on any of these observations one thing we can agree on—THE CHURCH IN THE FIRST CENTURY DIDN'T HAVE THESE. And amazingly they did what we haven't done or aren't doing and that's preach the Gospel to every creature—even with all this and more. How can we account for this?

Actually, it's not "WHAT they had" rather it's WHO they had. Remember Acts 4:13? *"Now when they SAW the boldness of Peter and John, and perceived they were uneducated and untrained men, they marveled. And they realized that they HAD BEEN WITH JESUS."*

Because of the WHO—Jesus Christ—the WHAT automatically steps into the spotlight. The WHAT is the GOSPEL. The Gospel is the message wrapped in the love of God for the entire world (Cf. John 3:16). The Gospel is the Good News about the birth, life, death, burial, resurrection, the ascension of Christ, and His return (Cf. 1 Corinthians 16:1-6; Romans 1:14-16).

The word "Gospel" is the Greek word *euagglion* and basically means *"Good new, tidings, word, a message."* It is used in various forms approximately 75 times in Scripture.

The Gospel is the only message which, if presented, understood and obeyed and lived faithfully, has the power to save a lost person (Cf. Romans 1:14-16; 10:10-17). This is what the first-century church had going for it—the one message—the cross of Christ and commitment to it. *"Then Jesus said to His disciples, 'If ANYONE DESIRES to come AFTER ME, let him DENY himself, and take up a CROSS, and FOLLOW Me'"* (Matthew 16:24).

No matter how talented or deep his knowledge may be, no preacher or a messenger of Christ can save a person with cute illustrations, personal stories, and scare tactics; these CANNOT save a person—only the Gospel can save. Sadly, I've attended many meetings advertised as "Gospel Meetings" where the Gospel was not preached. In some cases it was hinted at or tacked on quickly at the end of a long and drawn out message appropriate for the edification of the saved.

If we want EXPLOSIVE conversions as we read about in Acts we need to get back to the basics of preaching and teaching the Gospel.

FOR THOUGHT AND DISCUSSION

1. What are the most conversions your congregation has had in a year? How did it happen?

2. Why has the number of yearly conversions declined?

3. What are you personally doing to increase conversions?

4. What major lessons do we learn from the Book of Acts?

5. How has the Gospel been neglected?

6. How does Luke 8:11-15 relate to conversions?

7. What additional observations do you have?

8. How will you intentionally apply this lesson to your life? Why?

ENDEAVORING MISSION

On June 16, 1858, In Springfield, Illinois, Abraham Lincoln accepted the Republican Party's nomination to become a U.S Senator. The issue of slavery was raging in the nation. With a deep concern about the issue which has been supported by the opposing Democratic Party, Lincoln gave a 30-minute speech from which one line has been remembered. *"A house divided against itself cannot stand."*

Many people may not know that Lincoln's famous line was taken from the remarks of Jesus Christ. When Jesus was accused of trying to serve Satan and God, which wasn't possible, In Matthew 12:25 we read: *"But Jesus knew their thoughts, and said to them, 'Every kingdom divided against itself is brought to desolation, and every city or house divided against itself will not stand."*

DIVISION! SPLIT! These two words have through the centuries been responsible for the destruction of families, groups, nations, and churches. No wonder DIVISION is one of the things God HATES: *"These six things the Lord HATES, yes seven is an abomination to Him: A proud look, a lying tongue, hands that shed innocent blood, a heart that devises wicked plans, feet that are swift in running to evil, a false witness who speaks lies, and one who causes DIVISION among brethren"* (Proverbs 6:16-19).

After man's expulsion from the Garden of Eden because of disobedience, in one context or another, in one group of people or another, these things God hates, especially DIVISION has been occurring. A study of Judges, I & II Samuel, I & 11 Kings, I & II Chronicles, and the Prophets reveal the continual divisions which occurred in the Nation of Israel. The ultimate one divided the nation into the Northern and Southern kingdoms. Refer back to our study of how God's eternal mission was to bring ALL NATIONS into one "spiritual nation"—the church under His *"reign and rule"—kingdom (Cf. Isaiah 2:2-4).*

DIVISIONS AMONG CHRISTIANS

In writing to the church in Corinth, Paul exposed their division: *"Now I PLEAD with you, BRETHREN, by the name of our Lord Jesus Christ, that you ALL speak the same things, and that there be NO DIVISION among you, but that you be PERFECTLY JOINED TOGETHER in the same mind and in the same judgment. For it has been reported to me concerning you brethren, by those of Chloe's household, that there are DIVISIONS (i.e. contentions) AMONG YOU" (1 Corinthians 1:10, 11; Cf. 1:12-16; 3:4-8).* Read the book to see the many things they were divided over and how love was the solution (Cf. chapter 13).

If you have been a Christian for a few years, maybe even months, you have been made aware of, or maybe were affected by, a split or division in a congregation. In my years as a Christian, I have seen or heard about more splits and division than I care to remember. Sadly, I have a list of over 120 issues such as doctrines, opinions, personalities, property, money, ethnicity, politics, programs, leadership, strife and other issues which have caused confusion, unrest, rejection, division and splits in congregations.

It's amazing how Satan can use anything no matter how small, un-biblical, or ridiculous it may be to create confusion and spits in the family of God. An interesting and important thing to note relative to conflict, disagreement, etc. is that congregations such as Corinth or the five churches in Asia weren't encouraged or commanded to split off into another group; rather they were told to correct the issues in the spirit of love and family. It is true of every congregation: "A con-gregation divided against itself cannot stand" AT LEAST IN GOD'S FA-VOR. **He hates division.**

The Psalmist paints this beautiful picture relative to how God views unity among His people in: *"BEHOLD, how good and how pleasant it is for BRETHREN to dwell together in UNITY! It is like the precious oil upon the head, running down on the beard, the beard of Aaron, run-ning down on the edge of his garment. It is like the dew of Hermon, descending upon the mountains of Zion; for there the Lord com-manded the blessing—Life forevermore" (Psalm 133:1-3).*

In commenting on how God and a prophet must be in agreement if God's will is to be accomplished, Amos records this question: *"Can two walk together, unless they are in agreement?" (Amos 3:3).* These prin-ciples are true in every situation—marriage, politics, business, etc.

DIVERSITY FACTORS CONTRIBUTION TO DIVISION

I encourage you to refresh your awareness of the great diversity God intended to bring together in ONE BODY—the *ekklesia*—as ONE family unit living in the UNITY of the Spirit. From different nations, religions, beliefs, habits, diets, ethics, opinions, experiences, values, emotions, fears, habits, etc. will be formed into ONE household for the Lord (1 Timothy 3:15).

Diversity is one of the reasons why Paul said: *"For though I am free from all men, I have made myself a SERVANT to ALL, that I might win the more; and to the Jews I became as a Jew, that I might win the Jews; to those under the law, as under the law, that I might win those who are under the law; to those who are without law, as without law (not being without law toward God, but under law toward Christ), that I might WIN those who are without law; to the weak I became as weak, that I might win the weak. I HAVE BECOME ALL THINGS TO ALL MEN, THAT I MIGHT, BY ALL MEANS, SAVE SOME. **Now, this I DO for the gospel's sake, that I may be partaker of it with you"** (1 Corinthians 9:19-23).

No, Paul didn't partake of their sins or wrongdoings. He was sensitive to their sinful state and how God's grace was given for their salvation too. Paul didn't breath out condemnation against everything that was wrong in their lives. He shared the Gospel as the solution to their four major problems; their (1) sin problem, (2) life problem, (3) grave (death) problem, and (4) eternity (heaven and hell) problem.

They could come into the family of God as adopted Children where all their diversities, the wrongs would be defeated, and the rights used in their glorification of God and growing in the core **E's.** It would be a spiritual *E Pluribus Union.*

THE ENDEAVORING MISSION

Whether it's in a family, business, a team, among friends, etc. trying to maintain unity can be a challenge. When we look at the challenges presented by the amazing diversity which existed in the congregations of the First Century, it seems impossible from a human standpoint. But with God, it is not only possible but COMMANDED.

To the church in Ephesus had elders (Acts 20:20-28); and later charged with leaving their *"first love" (Revelation 2:4, 5),* Paul charged them to work on their diversity issues and create UNITY.

Ephesians 4:1-3: *I, therefore, the prisoner of the Lord, BESEECH you to walk worthy of the calling with which you were called, with all lowliness and gentleness, with longsuffering, bearing with ONE ANOTHER in love. ENDEAVORING to keep the UNITY of the SPIRIT in the bond of PEACE."*

Notice the 10 SPECIFIC qualities, attitudes and behaviors Paul is commanding and calling to their attention in their efforts to maintain UNITY:

(1) Remember it is an apostle of Christ who is writing to them.

(2) He is BESEECHING them (Encouraging, admonishing, begging).

(3) To walk WORTHY (to honor their position in Christ).

(4) In all LOWLINESS (To maintain an attitude of humility).

(5) With GENTLENESS (Do not be harsh, ugly, or unkind).

(6) With LONGSUFFERING (Be patient with your brethren).

(7) BEARING with one another (You are family—not strangers).

(8) ENDEAVORING to keep (It will take deliberate effort).

(9) The UNITY of the Spirit (It's not some manmade rules, etc.).

(10) In the bond of PEACE (Not confusion, conflict, arguing, etc.).

Once these attitudes, beliefs, and behaviors are understood and practiced, the platform for working on UNITY is in place. Let's notice the second part of the unity platform.

Ephesians 4:4-7: *"There is ONE body and ONE Spirit, just as you were called in ONE hope off your calling; ONE Lord, ONE faith, ONE baptism, ONE God and Father of all, is above all, and through all, in you all. But to each ONE of us, GRACE was given according to the measure of Christ's gift."*

Notice how the number **1** is referenced **8** times in verses 4-7, which is the key to maintaining UNITY in the church:

(1) *There is ONE body (This the body of Christ, the church, Colossians 1:18; to which members are added by God (1 Corinthians 12:18).*

(2) *There is ONE Spirit (This is the Holy Spirit who is given to the obedient, Acts 2:38; 5:32; He bears witness that we are sons of God).*

(3) *There is ONE hope (We are saved by hope, Romans 8:24)*

(4) *There is ONE Lord (Jesus Christ is the only Lord and Potentate, 1 Timothy 6:14, 15).*

(5) *There is ONE faith (There is only one faith that justifies, Romans 5:1; Hebrews 11:6).*

(6) *There is ONE baptism (It is an immersion in water for the remission of sins, Acts 2:38; 22:16; and into Christ, Galatians 3:27).*

(7) *There is ONE God (We meet Him in Genesis 1:1, in creation, Romans 1:19-25, etc.).*

(8) *There is ONE grace (This is God's gift of salvation, which is not a work, but free, Ephesians 2:8-10).*

According to these passages, there are 18 factors related to the church, and each Christian, which must be acknowledged, believed and practiced in order to maintain the UNITY OF THE SPIRIT.

FOR THOUGHT AND DISCUSSION

1. Why is unity so vital to the mission of the church?
2. Why is unity in a congregation so important?
3. Discuss "A house divided cannot stand."
4. Why were there so many diversities in the Corinth church?
5. What have you witnessed as a division in a congregation?
6. Have you advocated splitting a church? Why?
7. Why is attitude a major key in endeavoring to keep the unity of the Spirit?
8. What additional observations do you have?
9. How will you intentionally use this lesson?

ENCOUNTERING THE ENEMY OF THE CHURCH'S MISSION

There's a fable about one brother in a congregation borrowing a large sum of money from another brother. The due date for repayment came and the borrower had an excuse for not repaying his debt. This when on for several months—the borrower offering excuses and trying to avoid contact with the lender. The lender tried to use Matthew 18:15-20, which didn't work. The lenders thought about taking the borrower to court but changed his mind because of 1 Corinthians 6:1-11.

In time and uncontrollable frustration, the lender thought of something he could do that might motivate the borrower to repay his debt. It was on a Sunday morning just before services started, when the lender knew the borrower would be seated on his front pew as usual, that the lender rushed out of a front door in the auditorium dressed like the traditional portrayal picture of the Devil in a red suit, forked tail, horns, and a pitchfork. In a loud voice, he said, "If you don't pay brother Doe the money you owe him I'm going to cast you into hell."

The borrower stood up and in a trembling but confident voice said, "Now wait a minute, Satan! I have been a member of this church for

25 years, served on various committees, taught Bible classes, visited the sick, defended the truth, and attended all the services and fellowships. But I want you to know, and remember, that I have been on your side all along."

While we may smile at this fable there is at the same time the sad awareness that there are some on the pews who are, by their actions or lack of actions, playing into the hands of Satan, thus ENEMIES of the God's mission for the church. A prime Bible example of this behavior is Judas. Remember he was eating and fellowshipping with Jesus and the rest of the Apostles when *"Satan entered him"* *(Matthew 26:17-25).*

Jesus made it clear where one's enemies may exist: *"[A]nd a man's enemies WILL BE those of HIS OWN household"* *(Matthew 10:36; Cf. Micah 7:6).* Therefore, since the church is *"THE HOUSE OF GOD"* *(1 Timothy 3:15),* we can expect enemies to exist in the community *(ekklesia)* of Christ.

Satan is more than a mythological character who comes out around Halloween to scare small children as they "trick or treat" neighbors. He is a money maker—big business—as costumed actors portray him dressed in red having glowing red eyes, a forked tail, carrying a pitchfork, breathing out ugly steam, and horns on his head. Satan is in one of his most powerful positions when he convinces us that he is only a joke, not real, that he doesn't really exist.

When I was in the Navy we were trained to recognize our enemies and by so doing we could protect our own lives, duty station, and nation. This required hours of studying the identity of enemies.

SATAN IS ON A MISSION TO SEEK AND DESTROY

As soldiers of Christ (2 Timothy 2:1-3), we must be prepared and constantly on guard as we *"fight the good fight of faith" (1 Timothy 6:11, 12). We must not "allow Satan to get or have an advantage over us" (2 Corinthians 2:11).*

In Acts 5:1-11, we have the account of Ananias and Sapphira allowing Satan to motivate them to lie both to God and the church. The lie brought the immediate death penalty and the first record of a funeral among church members. Satan isn't outside of the church throwing stones, he is roaming around among the saints *"like a roaring lion SEEKING whom he may devour" (1 Peter 5:8).* Remember, he even had the nerve to approach Christ—God in the flesh (Matthew 4:1-6). We must not think for one moment that he will spare or exempt us; especially if we are LIVING FAITHFULLY (Revelation 2:10).

SOME OF SATAN'S TACTICS AGAINST OUR MISSION

The more we are ignorant of Satan devices the better are his chances of taking advantage of us and defeating our efforts in pursuing the mission of the church, or hinder us from going back to the basics.

Here are some Scriptural references to how Satan tries to hinder and destroy our mission:

1. He tries to **steal** the word out of our hearts (Luke 8:12).

2. He tries to **hinder** us from doing our mission (1 Thessalonians 2:17, 18).

3. He is a **liar** (Genesis 3:4; John 4:43-47).

4. He tries to perform pseudo **miracles and signs** (2 Thessalonians 2:9).

5. He is a dogmatic **accuser** of Christians (Revelation 12:9, 10).

6. He is a bold **confronter** and **tempter**—Jesus is an example (Matthew 4:1-6).

7. He is the **ruler** of this world (John 12:31).

8. He is **vicious** like a lion (1 Peter 5:8).

9. He is a **blinder** (2 Corinthians 4:4).

10. He is a **murderer** (John 8:44).

11. He is a **sifter** (Luke 12:31).

12. He is a **sower** of deadly seed (words) (Matthew 13:36-43).

13. He **fills** the heart with lies (Acts 5:3).

14. He **"believes"** there is a God (James 2:19; Job 1 & 2).

15. He is a **tactician** (Matthew 4:11: he left only for "a season").

These 15 attributes and actions of Satan must be known, believed, and a defense prepared against them. We MUST NOT be *"ignorant of his devices."* If we are he will detour, detain, and defeat us as we seek to fulfill our biblical mission by going back to the basics, etc.

HOW TO ENCOUNTER THE ENEMY OF OUR MISSION

Here is how Paul described the nature of the spiritual warfare we are continually engaged in as soldiers of Christ:

Ephesians 6:10-13: *"Finally, my brethren, be strong in the Lord and in the power of His might. Put on the whole armor of God that you may be able to stand against the WILES of the DEVIL. For we do not wrestle against flesh and blood, but against principalities, against powers, against the rulers of darkness of this age, against spiritual hosts of wickedness in the heavenly places."*

Here is how Paul commands that, as soldiers of Christ, we dress and arm ourselves to fight and win the spiritual war we're engaged in.

Ephesians 6:13-18: *"Therefore take up the whole armor of God, that you may be able to withstand the EVIL DAY, and having done all, to stand. STAND therefore, having girded your waist with TRUTH, having put on the breastplate of RIGHTEOUSNESS, and having shod your feet with the PREPARATION of the GOSPEL of peace; above ALL, taking the shield of FAITH with which you will be able to quench ALL the fiery darts of the WICKED ONE. And the helmet of SALVATION, and the sword of the Spirit, which is the WORD of God; PRAYING always with ALL PRAYER and SUPPLICATION in the Spirit, being WATCHFUL to this end with ALL PERSEVERANCE and SUPPLICATION for ALL the saints."*

Go back and count the keywords I have placed in capital letters; there are 15. Each one in the context is commanded relative to the ways and means we must use in order to fight and win the battle against evil—Satan and his demonic actions through human beings here on earth—sinful behaviors.

We need to take these 15 basic tactics and return to the basics of making them a foundation plank in our spiritual training to identify, engage, and defeat the enemy. Sadly, some have never gone through the "basic boot camp" where these first principles of warfare were taught.

ADDITIONAL REASONS OUR ENEMY WILL NOT WIN

Jesus didn't leave heaven, travel to earth, reside in a womb for 9 months, squeeze out of the birth canal, be threatened with death as an infant, grow up, be ridiculed and rejected, to be tried illegally, suffer and die on a tree, to be buried in a borrowed tomb in order to sponsor or pull off a failure and be defeated by Satan. Never!

Here are some additional reasons why we know God's family, His *ekklesia, called out community* will not be defeated eternally. Read the end of the Story—Book of Revelation—"hallelujah we win!" Study prayerfully and carefully the following basic truths about why we know we are MORE THAN CONQUERORS in Christ (Romans 8:1, 37):

1. **1 John 3:8:** *"He who sins is of the DEVIL, for the DEVIL has sinned from the beginning. For this PURPOSE the Son of God was manifested, that He might DESTROY the works of the DEVIL."*

2. **Hebrews 2:14:** *"Inasmuch then as the children have partaken of flesh and blood, He Himself likewise share in the same, that through DEATH He might DESTROY him who had POWER of DEATH, that is, the DEVIL."*

3. **Colossians 2:15:** *"Having DISARMED **principalities and powers**, He made a public spectacle of them, TRIUMPHING over them in it."*

4. **In Mark 3:22-28,** Jesus makes it clear that He has the POWER to enter Satan's house and bind him. *"No one can enter a strong man's house and plunder his goods, unless he FIRST binds the strong man, and then shall he plunder his house"* *(3:27).*

5. **James 4:6, 7:** *"But He gives more grace. Therefore He says: 'God resists the proud, but gives more grace to the humble.' Therefore SUBMIT to God. RESIST THE DEVIL and he will FLEE from you."*

6. **In Matthew 6:13,** we are told to pray for deliverance from Satan: *"And do not lead us into temptation, but DELIVER us from the EVIL ONE…"*

7. **Revelation 20:10:** *"The DEVIL who deceived them, was cast into the LAKE OF FIRE AND BRIMSTONE where the beast and the false prophets are. And they will be TORMENTED day and night FOREVER and EVER."*

The truths we have covered about ENCOUNTERING the enemy—Satan—is one of the major **E's** of the church and her mission. These form a BACK TO BASIC foundations for learning and applying God's WORD for winning the spiritual warfare we are perpetually engaged in. As soldiers of Christ, we must never forget these basics, snooze, or fall asleep while on duty—which is 24-7-365 (Cf. 2 Timothy 2:1-3).

FOR THOUGHT AND DISCUSSION

1. Why do some Christians say they believe there is a Devil but live like he doesn't exist?

2. Why has a study of Satan been neglected (or has it)?

3. How have the jokes, movies, cartoons, and Halloween costumes reduced any serious concept of Satan?

4. Why would a parent dress a child in an everyday T-shirt with "I'm a little Devil" printed on the front?

5. Discuss "If the enemy can convince us that he doesn't exist he is already winning."

6. When was the last time you engaged in a basic study of Satan and his tactics? Why?

7. How do all church problems, issues, and conflicts relate to the activity of Satan? How is he able to get by with his efforts?

8. How do you resist the Devil? When do you resist him?

9. What additional observations do you have about this lesson?

10. How will you intentionally use this lesson in your life and ministry?

ENDURING FAITHFULLY TO THE END

Have you ever heard this colloquialism, "It ain't over till (until) the fat lady sings"? (Yes, I know today it's politically incorrect). Historically the phrase was used to reference the stereotypically overweight Sopranos of the Opera. In the '70s, on Monday Night Football, Don Meredith, a former Dallas Cowboy quarterback, as a TV commentator would say when the game was close and almost over, "It ain't over till the fat lady sings." Yogi Berra, a baseball player, and the manager said, *"It ain't over till it's over."*

What does this have to do with going back to basics and studying our **E's** mission? Here's what it has to do with our mission. **It isn't over until our lives on earth end in death with our last breaths are drawn in FAITHFULNESS.** His messages to the church in Ephesus was they had left their first love, Jesus commanded:

Revelation 2:10: *"Do not fear any of those things which you are about to SUFFER. Indeed the DEVIL is about to throw some of you into PRISON, that you may be TESTED, and you will have TRIBULATION ten days. BE FAITHFUL UNTIL DEATH, and I WILL give you the CROWN OF LIFE."*

Paul reminded the Romans that the Christian life was begun, continued, and consummated through living by faith (Romans 1:16, 17).

WHAT IS FAITH?

It is elementary that in order to live faithfully until death when all our trials on earth will be over, that we know what faith is. Linguistically faith is defined as follows:

Webster: English: *Faith: 1. a. allegiance to duty as a person—loyalty, b. fidelity to one's promise, the sincerity of intention 2. b. belief and trust and loyalty to God, b.* belief in the traditional doctrines of religion, c. a firm belief in something for which there is no proof.

Greek: *Faith: the root word for faith is the noun Pistis, and the Greek verb which is translated believe is Pistuea. Faith means a firm belief, persuasion, assurance, conviction, faithfulness, etc. Believe may not be as dedicated.* For example, many people believe Jesus lived and was who He claimed to be, even the Savior of the world. But they will not trust him or obey His word. That's just "mental assent", which is the kind of belief the Devil has (CF. James 2:24).

Biblical FAITH, without which we cannot please God (Hebrew 11:6), is putting your eternal destiny in God's hand and is based on accepting the "blood of Christ" as the atonement for your sins (Matthew 26:28; Romans 5:1-12); and living faithfully every day (2 Corinthians 5:7).

Hebrews 11:1-40: Here is how God defines and illustrates what faith is. It is not only a belief in and about something or someone; it is also ACTIONS based on those beliefs. It starts with, *"Now faith is the*

SUBSTANCE of things HOPED for, the EVIDENCE of things not seen" (11:1).

In the rest of the chapter, we have historical examples of how people demonstrated their faith by their actions (Take time to go and read them). In chapter 12 we are told that the faithful discussed in chapter 11 are our examples: *"Therefore we also, since we are surrounded by so great a cloud of witnesses, let us lay aside every weight, and sin which so easily ensnares us, and let us run with ENDURANCE the race that is set before us, looking to Jesus, the author and finisher of our FAITH... (Hebrews 12:1, 2; 5:8, 9).*

We must not forget as we go back to the basics that all the previous elements of our mission depend on FAITH. We must not forget what James wrote relative to having only a mouthing of belief in God—"saying the creed—but not DOING the deed" (Cf. James 1:21-27).

James 2:17-20: *"Thus also FAITH by ITSELF (mental assent), if it does not have WORKS (actions), is DEAD. But someone will say, 'You have faith, and I have works.' SHOW me your FAITH without your WORKS (actions), and I will SHOW you my faith by my works (actions). You BELIEVE that there is one God. You do well. Even the demons BELIEVE (mental assent)—and TREMBLE! But do you want to KNOW, O foolish man, that faith WITHOUT Works (actions) is DEAD?"*

The apostle Peter makes it clear that because God has given us ALL THINGS that pertain to life and godliness, we must be ACTIVELY supplying certain VIRTUES out of our FAITH to our daily spiritual lives (2

Peter 1:3, 4). The verses which follow should leave no doubt that the apostle is commanding an ACTIVE faith, not a TALKING belief.

2 Peter 1:5-8: *"But also for this very reason, giving all DILIGENCE, Add to your (i.e. supply out of) FAITH virtue, to virtue knowledge, to knowledge self-control, to self-control perseverance, to perseverance godliness, to godliness brotherly kindness, and to brotherly kindness love. **For he who lacks these THINGS is shortsighted, even to blindness, and has FORGOTTEN that he was cleansed from his old sins."*** Peter makes it clear that ACTIVE FAITH is a producer of spiritual attitudes and behaviors.

KEYS TO DEVELOPING AN ENDURING FAITH

From the above Scriptures from James and Peter, it is clear that enduring faith—faith that lasts—must be ACTIVE. It takes what is mouthed as BELIEF—"I believe there is only ONE God"—and puts it into acts of obedience. Here are some basic keys to developing and sustaining an enduring faith.

FIRST, remember we are commanded to ENDURE, also remember that the Greek word *katereo* means several behavioral qualities, *"to hold up, to hold out, be strong, firm, remaining, remain under, etc.* Here are some verses: **Mark 13:13**, *"And you will be hated by all for My name's sake. But he who ENDURES to the end shall be saved"* (Cf. Mark 4:17). **1 Peter 2:19,** *"For this is commendable, if because of conscience toward God one ENDURES grief, suffering wrongfully."*

SECOND, it is avoiding the practices of the Pharisees who were guilty of SAYING good words and giving commands but not DOING them. Here is Jesus' condemnation of the SAYERS but not DOERS: *"…The scribes and the Pharisees sit in Moses' seat. Therefore whatever they TELL you to OBSERVE, that OBSERVE and **DO**, but DO NOT according to their works; for they **SAY** and **do not do**"(Matthew 23:1-3)*.

THIRD, remember that the blessings of heaven and eternal life come after we have lived a faithful spiritual life right to the END: *"[R]eceiving the END OF YOUR FAITH—the salvation of your SOULS" (1 Peter 1:9). "… Be FAITHFUL until DEATH, and I will give you the crown of life" (Revelation 2:10)*.

FOURTH, keep the shield of faith in place in order to guard your heart: *"[A]bove all, taking the SHIELD of FAITH with which you are able to Quench all the fiery darts of the WICKED ONE" (Ephesians 6:16)*.

FIFTH, never forget God's definition and description of what faith is: *"Now FAITH IS the substance of things HOPED for the EVIDENCE of things not seen. For BY IT the elders obtained a good report" (Hebrews 11:1)*. Study this verse carefully.

SIXTH, continually remember that the Christian walk was begun in faith and culminates in faith (Romans 1:17). And *"Without faith, it is IMPOSSIBLE to please God" (Hebrews 11:6)*.

SEVENTH, make it a scheduled habit to frequently read Hebrews chapter 11. It will continually help you remember the faith which pleases God is an active faith, not just a "talking a good fight faith."

EIGHTH, never forget the example of a Christian living and dying in the faith which was demonstrated by Stephen in the first-century church. The account of his sermon and death is recorded in Acts 7. Proof of his ENDURING faith is recorded for us: *"And they stoned Stephen as he was calling on God and saying, 'Lord Jesus, receive my spirit.' Then he knelt down and cried out with a loud voice, 'Lord, do not charge them with this sin.' And when he had said this, he fell asleep"* (Acts 7:59, 60). **Will I, will you, will all of us be able to endure to the end like Stephen? YES! If we LIVE BY FAITH.**

FOR THOUGHT AND DISCUSSION

1. Why is faith the key to believing and doing the basic **E's**?

2. How have the words *"believe"* and *"faith"* been misunderstood and applied by some?

3. How can *believing* something be limited by *mental assent only?*

4. How does the example of demons believing in God prove that *mental and verbal assent* is not active or doing faith?

5. What are some things Christians have to ENDURE today? Why?

6. How have you, starting with your "infant faith", built it to the "mature faith" you now have?

7. If you were asked to develop a faith-building curriculum where would you start? How would you proceed?

8. What additional observations do you have?

9. How will you intentionally apply this lesson to your life and ministry?

10. How will you follow up on this study? What subjects?

BACK TO BASICS SEMINAR OR MEETING

The author, Dr. J.J. Turner, can be contacted for information about scheduling the **Back to Basics** series either in a seminar, workshop, coaching leadership sessions, or meeting.

Dr. J.J. Turner
400 Lake Dow Road
McDonough, GA. 30252
770-957-8611
drjjturrner@gmail.com
www.jeremiahinstitute.com